CW01021845

A L
Well Lived

A Life Well Lived

Della Brookshaw

BRAMBLEWOOD
PUBLISHING

Bramblewood Publishing
3, Bramblewood Close
Overton-on-Dee, North Wales, LL13 0HJ

www.bramblewoodpublishing.org
Bramblewoodpublishing@outlook.com

© Della Mary Brookshaw, 2024

All rights reserved. No part of this publication may be reproduced or transmitted in any form or by any means, electronic or mechanical, including photocopying, recording or any information storage or retrieval system, without prior permission from the publishers.

First published by Bramblewood Publishing, 2024.
First edition: May 2024. This impression: September 11th, 2024.

ISBN: 978-0995499638

Cover design: Robert J Davies, inc painting by J. Glazebrook

Designed and typeset in 12pt Palatino Linotype by Robert J Davies
Printed and bound in Great Britain

ABOUT THE AUTHOR:

Della Mary Brookshaw was born Della Mary Cooke in 1938 to a farming family in Staffordshire and grew up surrounded by pigs and cattle and a shire horse used for ploughing. She vividly recalls the war years which, living on a farm, weren't as harsh as for people in the towns. The Cookes could slaughter their own pigs for bacon and ham and had plentiful supplies of potatoes and vegetables from their own fields.

Della has happy memories of growing up with her brother Peter, six years her senior, and a small but close-knit circle of friends. There was great fun to be had playing hide and seek in the farmhouse and barns and looking after the pet goat. But tragedy struck when she was 12: her father died aged just 48.

Della had to learn to be resilient and get on with life. She did so, becoming a skilled cook along the way – something she enjoys to this day. In the late 1950s she won dozens of awards at local agricultural shows, and in 1962 was featured in a national magazine article featuring her cookery and skill at preserving fruit and vegetables in jams and chutneys. By this time she was married to farmer Anthony Brookshaw and with him, transformed The Plassey near Wrexham from a rundown dairy farm into the hugely successful caravan park and retail centre we know today.

Sadly, while writing this autobiography, Della lost her 87-year-old husband after more than 60 years of marriage. But he told her, towards the end, to get on with life and enjoy herself which is what she continues to do. She still lives at The Plassey and although her son John and daughter-in-law Sarah are now in charge, Della lends a hand with day-to-day tasks and enjoys meeting and chatting to the caravanners and shoppers, many of whom have been coming to The Plassey for years.

ACKNOWLEDGEMENTS:

I would like to express my profound thanks to everyone, including my wonderful family, for making my life so joyful and filled with fun and inspiration – and also to Robert Davies for helping me compile my memories into this book.

This book is dedicated to:

My son John, daughters Julie and Jane and also daughter-in-law Sarah and son-in-law Robert, grandsons Ben and William and granddaughter Zara.

I love you all. x

Della as a young child with the carthorse at Old Peel Farm in the 1940s.

The cow Della is sitting on in the photograph on the back cover, when she was aged about six, was named after her and the farm by her father: a pedigree Friesian dairy cow called Peel Della.

The front cover incorporates a watercolour of The Plassey painted in 1977 by the late Mrs Jean Glazebrook, a talented artist who lived in the nearby villages of Overton-on-Dee and Knolton Bryn.

CONTENTS

1	*Early years*	13
2	*End of an era*	32
3	*Growing up*	41
4	*The Plassey story begins!*	50
5	*Becoming parents*	60
6	*A new direction*	72
7	*The Plassey takes shape*	80
8	*Stormy times*	93
9	*From cow shed to restaurant*	102
10	*John prepares to take the helm*	116
11	*Memorable moments*	128
12	*Holidays*	135
13	*Parties and celebrations*	149
14	*Recent times*	164
15	*Sad death of Tony*	171
16	*Life goes on*	175
	Appendix: A little more about Tony	192
	Postscript	209

Mrs Della Mary Brookshaw

PREFACE

It was just over four years ago, in January 2020, that I decided it was time to write a memoir of my life. I have had a varied life so I thought, why not tell people about it? And I have many photographs so why not include some of them to help tell the story? So I started to put pen to paper.

I have always regretted not asking my parents and aunts and uncles about their lives and felt that it was very important as we get older and we think back about our past. When we're younger it doesn't bother us but when you get into your 80s, you then look back and want other people, especially the family, to learn about your experiences and how everything started – growing up and where we were born, where we went to school, what our careers were and how we lived during the war. Lots of things happened which probably they never knew about.

This book is therefore intended to be for the benefit (if they regard it as such) of my family and also for any friends who may be interested.

So here goes, and pleasant reading . . .

Della Brookshaw
May, 2024.

CHAPTER ONE

EARLY YEARS

WHEN my mother was expecting me, my father went to the local petrol station in Audley, Staffordshire, and a friend from a neighbouring farm cycling past shouted across to him, 'has May had the baby yet?' And father shouted back, 'yes, twins this morning.'

The neighbour, who had recently had a baby herself, pedalled back at full speed to collect extra baby clothes for my mother because she realised that she wouldn't have enough clothes for two.

She then rode down to my mother who was hanging clothes on the line and said to her, 'I saw Arthur this morning and he said you had had twins. I've got these two bags of clothes as you won't have enough for two babies.' My mother replied, 'yes, we had twin *calves* this morning!' They laughed together. This is what they did in the countryside – sharing jokes. Father was a great joker.

I wasn't a twin, of course. My elder brother, James Peter Cooke, was born in 1932 – six years before me.

I was born on 27th October, 1938, at Old Peel Farm, Audley, Staffordshire. Mother chose my name Della, which is quite an unusual name. It is derived from my grandmother's name Evalyn Adela Harris.

At the time of my birth, my father, Mr Arthur Cooke, was a farmer and we occupied a farm of 180 acres which was rented from a local farmer called Mr Sammy Adams.

My mother, May Harris, married my father in 1932 at St Margaret's Church, Wrenbury, Cheshire. Before her marriage she lived at Yew Tree Farm, Wrenbury, with her parents, Mr and Mrs James Harris. She was the eldest child and had two brothers, Jim and Gerald.

May and Arthur Cooke on their wedding day in 1932.

On leaving boarding school she worked at home helping on the farm, which was the norm in those days, making cheese and cooking for the family. Her mother Evalyn was a very good cook and taught my own mother many skills which I also inherited, along with a love of cooking.

Having been born just before the outbreak of war, I can remember as a child the worrying time my parents had and coping with the terrifying sound of bombs dropping during the many nights of the long war. I can remember going down into the shelters when I was at the local school in Audley, although at the time we actually thought it was fun.

One night there was a very bad bombing in the Potteries where the Germans were trying to bomb a munitions factory. This we also thought was fun but it must have been very worrying for our parents. We were told to go into the cellar at home where Mother had a home-cooked chocolate cake waiting for us.

Della's Mother, May Harris.

Mother often took us outside to see the searchlights over Crewe, Cheshire, and to point out the 'elephants in the sky' which were, in fact, the barrage balloons used to defend against enemy aircraft.

I remember walking home from school and collecting streams of foil, which we later found out were dropped by our aircraft to confuse and deceive enemy radar systems.

Della as a toddler with a neighbour's boy and future childhood friend, Graham Brassington, being pushed by a maid.

Della as a young child at Old Peel Farm.

I recall that during the war, most food was rationed, although we were lucky, having the advantage of living on a farm where there was a plentiful supply of milk, eggs and cheese. We were allowed to kill one pig a year for our own consumption, so there was plenty of ham and bacon.

A slaughtered pig was an extremely valuable beast – even those who lived in the big cities would keep a porker in the backyard. Sometimes we would kill an extra one and get rid of all the blood quickly down the drain, it was all very secret. I had to be on the look out if anyone from the Ministry was coming up. The remaining pigs would all go to market.

There were no fridges then – the butcher would come and salt the meat and there was always a ham hanging up in the kitchen and father would slice pieces off. It would often be green, but it tasted okay.

We lived well during the war really. You learned to make the best of what you had. We used to have potatoes for the cattle dumped in a big mound – they used to pour purple liquid over them, to stop them being eaten by humans. I remember them covered in this purple liquid, which wasn't poisonous. Mother used to pick ones that weren't too discoloured and use them.

Sweets were rationed too, and my brother and I would save up our coupons to spend at the local sweet shop, so that on Christmas Eve we could have a midnight feast – one pound of sweets each on that special night

Brother James Peter Cooke, known as Peter, aged 14 months.

when Father Christmas visited us!

We were allowed to sleep in the same bedroom and so, on Christmas Eve when Father Christmas had been (we could feel the rustle on our feet at the bottom of the bed), we would wake each other up and enjoy all those sweets and open our presents, that was always a big delight.

Peter and Della, aged about 11 and 4.

The local sweet shop was run by Mrs Riley opposite the village school and she would give us the remains of a jar of sweets if they were all broken, as a
treat. We often used to go in and ask if there were
any remnants left.

Della, first on the left, top row, with her fellow school pupils.

During the war, my father used to grow potatoes
and fish and chip shops were only allowed a quota
of a couple of sacks of potatoes a month. Father was
friendly with people who had a fish and chip shop in
Hanley, Stoke-on-Trent. They would ask him if they
could have some.

So, when it was dark, he would go along with a
few sacks in the back of the car – I remember going
with him – and deliver them to the shop. In return
they would give him bags of surplus sugar and then
mother would take a sugar bag or two to the local

market in Hanley in return for extra sweets – where they made their own as they had great trouble getting enough sugar.

This sort of thing went on, you weren't allowed to have more than your quota, but there was a black market during the war, of course.

Despite the war, it was mainly a happy childhood for us and being in the countryside wasn't half as worrying as living in the city with all the bombing and fires which must have been terrible. We didn't see any of that in the countryside.

Of course, during the blackout while the war was on, you weren't supposed to have lights anywhere and there was a curfew in force. But Father and Mother would still hold parties. In winter, when it was dark, you had to be very careful in case a little chink of light came through the windows.

Peter as a young boy with Della and Peter's father Arthur Cooke and their grandfather Harry Cooke at Old Peel Farm, circa early 1930s.

The local policeman would come along the country lanes on his cycle and check. I remember one night the policeman knocking on the door. There were cars outside and he said, 'what's going on here' and Mother said, 'we're giving a party'. He said, 'but there are cars here and you're not supposed to go out at night.' So mother said, 'well come in and have a drink and meet everyone,' – so he came in and joined in the party!

We were also fortunate in that Father was never called up. Farmers were allowed to stay at home because they needed to provide food for the nation. But many young men would have been sent to fight, meaning there was a shortage of workers in agriculture. The Women's Land Army had been set up during the First World War to bring women into work to help replace the men called up. We had a land girl, as they were known, called Nancy who lived locally. She came to help on the farm for about 12 months. Land girls were always one of the family, really.

After the war, Nancy remained a family friend. She was always keen to come back and see us. She lived in Audley, about four miles away, and would probably cycle over – they used to cycle everywhere in those days. She would come and have a bit of lunch with us, Mother was always cooking for us and the family, and workers, and providing cups of tea. They were happy times, really. Nancy wasn't a farmer's daughter, not many of the land girls were, but they just loved working on the land.

Nancy was the only land girl we ever had, that I

can remember, but we had a farmworker who lived across the road in a little cottage, who used to come and help out.

Peter and Della on horseback with land girl, Nancy.

Then there was another man called Jim, who used to come most days. He loved to do the vegetable garden – we had lots of lovely vegetables – and usually he would arrive with a very colourful lollipop on a stick, we always used to look forward to this.

He used to have lunch with us but would always sit on another table in the kitchen, he would never sit around the table with the family. It's what happened with farmworkers, they always sat at another table, it was very strange.

I remember him sprinkling salt on his food – he would tap his spoon all over and Mother used to say to us, 'never do that, always put salt on the side of the plate. Don't copy Jim!'.

Jim became a family friend. I can remember going to his house one day. Mother always used to take him some mince pies. He lived on his own in a little terraced house in Audley I think, or a nearby village anyway.

One evening, in the dark, she walked down the little path to his house while I waited in the car. She could hear the sound of a violin and knocked on the door and went in. She came back crying. She said, 'I felt so sorry for him. He was on his own, playing a violin.' Mother was always very kind, especially looking after the older people.

Perhaps in part because workmen like Jim would often need feeding, meal times on the farm were always very regimented: 8.30am for breakfast, then 1pm for dinner. Tea would be at 5.30pm.

For breakfast, we would have porridge, bacon and eggs and toast and marmalade. Lunch – which we always called Dinner – would usually be a roast and there would always be pudding, often served with bread and butter! Tea was always sandwiches, cake and cups of tea. We always ate well and of course, it was hard work for farmers and labourers, so they needed good food. Farmers were up at half-past five so by breakfast time they had already been working for three hours.

When the war was over, on VE Day, Father took us in the car to Newcastle, the local town, to watch all the searchlights and dancing, it was wonderful and houses all had their lights on in celebration.

In those days, Audley was a close-knit farming community. I can remember six couples who were big friends of the family and Mother and Father used to have them over regularly for supper and dinner parties. They usually killed a cockerel to have for the meal and then play cards afterwards.

We would usually go to my grandmother's farm at Wrenbury for Christmas dinner, it would probably be a goose. All the family would gather there – Mother's brothers, wives and children. And we used to have a very big family party with all the cousins at Barthomley near Crewe with an aunt and uncle – my father's sister, husband and children.

On Boxing Night all the family would congregate together, mainly cousins, and we would have a big Christmas tree and a big meal and Father Christmas would come along with his bag of presents for our cousins. To this day we still have cousins' parties each year.

My parents were sociable people and well liked in the neighbourhood. Among our close friends were the Brassington family who lived about a mile up the road. Their son Graham was born about six months before me and we grew up together. That was handy in the countryside because you didn't have next-door neighbours.

Graham was my best friend really, and we often used to go to each other's houses. We didn't have a telephone in those days so when Mother said, 'Graham and Della will have to get together, say next Saturday', she would hang a blue sheet out of the

Della with neighbour and childhood best friend, Graham.

window so that his mother knew that Graham had arrived safely having walked along the road.

We were only about seven or eight at the time and it could get quite lonely unless you had somebody to play with.

Graham and I would play outside, sometimes on our bikes. I remember he had a three-wheeler bike which I wanted. One day, when visiting him, I decided that I wanted to take it home with me and Mother said, 'no, you're not having it, it belongs to Graham, it was his birthday present.'

So when I was on the back of Mother's bike I was so annoyed that I put my foot in the back of the spokes and cut it! I still didn't get Graham's bike! I was quite a determined little girl, I think. I liked to get my own way but didn't always manage to. I remember that quite plainly, I must have only been six or seven. Eventually I got a two-wheeler bike which I remember hadn't got any brakes! It must have been a second-hand one.

Then, one Christmas, Santa Claus had brought his toys and Mother said, 'go outside and have a look, Santa's been.' In the snow were two marks for his sleigh and he had brought me a brand new bicycle! They had to put wooden blocks on the pedals because my legs weren't long enough. In those days that's what they used to do. It was probably dangerous – we would fall off once or twice.

My brother would have his friends over and I used to play outside a lot with them. I remember on one hot summer's day, we decided to go swimming in the farm pond – well, we didn't actually swim. It was filthy dirty but we managed to go in there. It was where the cattle used to drink, it's a wonder we didn't catch some disease, but we survived!

I remember a cow calving at Old Peel Farm and Mother said, 'don't go near, we're calving a cow'. In those days, you didn't see that sort of thing, children were kept away from it as though it wasn't to be seen.

There was lots to do as a child. We used to play hide and seek in the lofts and sheds. I had a little goat which used to follow me everywhere, when I was about seven or eight. I used to call it Nanny. I remember coming back from school one day and went to look for Nanny and he was up in my bedroom chewing all my comics, which I wasn't very happy about!

Then very sadly one day he went into the shippon (cowshed) where they were milking the cows and a cow trod on him and broke his back. I went to the vets with him in the car and the vet said they couldn't do anything for him which really upset me.

However, I think farming broadens your outlook to accept the fact that animals don't always survive. Like when I had the children, Tony didn't really worry that much, to him it was like the birth of any animal. I remember feeling like I was a cow giving birth! You associate it with the same experience. The modern-day farmer has to be with them for the birth, it's a completely different outlook.

That said, cows calve the same and sheep lamb the same, it's just that it's more commercialised these days and farms may have hundreds of cows now, all mechanised with a lot more book-work involved – and health and safety is far more onerous today.

Della astride a cow at Old Peel Farm.

In other respects, life then, particularly on a farm out in the countryside, was very different from life today. We now take mains electricity for granted but at Old Peel Farm, we didn't even have a generator. We had to use oil lamps and candles for light. I can remember going to bed one day holding a paraffin lamp, which was lit. I fell over the Aladdin's stove at the top of the stairs. Mother heard this bang and came rushing up the stairs. The wick of the lamp was still alight so the first thing she did was blow it out.

Also, we didn't have a flush toilet at Old Peel Farm – we had to go down the garden path to the outside loo. Underneath, there were hens and you could hear them scratching! Once a month a man

used to come and collect the waste. I don't know what happened to it after that!

Della and cousin Ann Cooke (now Furnival) as bridesmaids. Ann went on to become godmother for Della's second daughter, Jane.

Father served as church warden at the local Audley church. He went regularly there and I remember the harvest festivals were wonderful. We always went to a friend's house afterwards for a meal – they held quite big celebrations at the church, and

the vicar Revd Lewis was a big friend of the family.

A photos of Della aged about nine or ten, on holiday in Llandudno circa 1940s.

Della and Peter with their mother and father in Llandudno.

Mother and Father used to invite him over for meals with a group of friends and many years later, he actually married Tony and me at Acton Church.

Father liked going to greyhound racing at Hanley. One time, the vicar of Audley said: 'I would love to go to a greyhound meeting.' Father agreed to take him along. In those days, clergymen were regarded very highly and didn't go anywhere where there was gambling! So when my Father took him, the vicar turned his collar round and wore a big scarf around his neck. But he was spotted!

A few weeks later somebody said to my father, 'wasn't that the vicar of Audley with you at the greyhound races?' Father replied, 'was it? Really? I don't know!' He always used to laugh about that.

I went to a funeral in Staffordshire recently and I went round the lanes which looked exactly the same as I remember them – and past Old Peel Farm. It has been altered quite a bit and painted white but it is still a farm and I can still recognise it. And the mill we used to go to is still there although it's been turned into a house now.

Seeing it brought back memories of going down to the mill in the horse-drawn cart with my father and my brother Peter. Father would take hundred-weight bags of grain for milling as feed for the cattle – wheat or barley – I'm not sure. It was quite an adventure, going to the top and watching the wheels grind the corn. It was probably only about quarter of a mile away and the motorway goes underneath now

– you don't really see it but you hear it.

It was a water mill where they had this huge tank of water which cascaded down to turn the wheel. I hated going past the tank because Peter always threatened to push me into it! So when I went past I would have to look the other way – he really frightened me with it! I remember the millers were Mr and Mrs Hodgkins. Looking back on my father's side of the family, they were nearly all millers.

I remember that the lanes used to be very dusty but they were tarmacked, because I can recall walking home from school and sometimes seeing the marks of the old steamrollers that used to do the threshing. They used to make indentations on the road – you would see these lines and we used to follow them to see where they had gone – the old steam engines I suppose were so heavy they would make these marks on the road.

Peter and Della, aged ten and four, respectively.

CHAPTER TWO

END OF AN ERA

OUR final winter at Old Peel farm was very harsh. In 1947 we had terrific snowfall and blizzards. There was a little lane called Cinder Lane between our farm and the Brassingtons a mile up the road. The hedges must have been about ten feet high and they were absolutely covered in snowdrifts right to the top.

We would take the sledge up and down the little slopes – it stuck in my memory because the snow was so deep. Of course, farming was especially hard work because the cattle had to stay inside. The water froze in the pipes and we had to heat the pipes to thaw them. Not having mains electricity then, we had to rely on oil lamps and paraffin heaters.

We also had an open fire – Father always put sticks in the oven each night to dry them out, then get up about six o'clock in the morning to light the fire with the dried sticks. It was an old-fashioned black-leaded fire grate with ovens at each side. The fire had to be lit early otherwise we wouldn't have hot water for washing in the morning.

We had lots of burst pipes that winter – it was a very hard winter but of course, being on a farm we had lots of wood to burn and coal which was plentiful as there were lots of coal mines around Stoke-on-Trent. We were never short of coal and wood for the fire.

We loved the snow, we thought it was exciting, having to dig out all the pathways – but I do remember the drifts, that was the biggest problem.

We were all very happy living at Old Peel Farm but on December 23rd, 1947, my parents had a letter from their landlord, Mr Adams, giving notice to vacate the farm by March 25th, 1948, as he needed it for his son to farm. We could not understand why it was for his son as he was only 16 years old at the time!

We found out subsequently that a new law was coming into force a few months later, where a tenancy agreement would give a tenant a three-generation contract (which is still the case today).

This came as a real shock to my parents as they were hoping their own son Peter would carry on the farm, where we had all been very happy. They had just three months to find another, where they could take their pedigree Friesian herd of milking cows. This was very difficult as there were very few farms suitable for herds of Friesians.

As the time drew nearer, my parents decided to sell the herd which father had worked so hard establishing, and move to a smaller, rented farm called Bradwell Hall Farm near Newcastle-under-Lyme.

This was not suitable for dairy farming which was why Father had to sell up before we moved there. It was meant to be a temporary move while we looked for a farm to buy but it was at a time when land was very expensive. I remember Jim, our vegetable gardener whom I mentioned in the previous chapter, crying when Father sold all the cattle at the farm sale. He came into the kitchen and said, 'I can't believe this is happening, those cows all going.'

Bradwell Hall Farm
in the 1940s.

I moved to the Lyme School in Newcastle-under-Lyme. It was a small, private school and convenient as my brother Peter was at Newcastle High School opposite. One day at playtime he called me over to his school playing field and asked if I would come and chat to him so I went over the road to the railings. He grabbed my long plaits and tied them to the railings! Our school bell went off for lessons and I was left stuck. A teacher was sent to unfasten me! I was very cross with him. Being six years older than me, Peter was always up to tricks and doing something mischievous. He loved playing pranks on me.

We had many happy times at Bradwell. Peter and I had lots of friends from school who loved to play in the outbuildings there and I also had school friends from the local villages who would come and play with me and we would often bake little cakes. We enjoyed playing in the bales of hay and making tunnels and dens.

A slightly blurred photo showing Michael, Roderick, Peter, Della, Julia, Christine and Janice on the farm tractor and below, Peter feeding the pigs.

We had the run of the large house and often played billiards and Monopoly with our friends. The house had about 20 rooms – I had my own little play room, we had so much freedom. We used to enjoy playing billiards with the boys but they didn't always like having us there, disrupting their games, and if we got on their nerves they would come and mess up our Monopoly game!

Peter was always annoying me and I was always annoying him. We had lots of arguments as brothers and sisters do but being a lot younger and a girl, Mother was quite protective of me.

The next chapter in my life was most upsetting for my family. On December 21st, 1949, my Father, after a short spell in hospital with angina, unexpectedly passed away. He was 48 years of age. Our world collapsed. It was such a blow to us all. I was only 12 years old and my brother 18. Mother was in a state of shock for a number of months. It changed our lives completely.

Father had been ill for a short while in hospital but was allowed to come home for Christmas which delighted us all. One afternoon, I was looking after him in bed. Mother and my brother had gone Christmas shopping.

When they returned I told Mother that Father had said to me that he felt fine. He had just wanted his light turning down a bit – in those days we just had oil lamps, as I mentioned before, we didn't have mains electricity – and a little pill which I gave him. That was about two hours earlier.

Mother went to see him. She came back and said, 'Father's gone, don't come in the bedroom.' That was a real shock, we hadn't expected it at all. Mother was

This is believed to be the last photograph of May and Arthur Cooke together, taken shortly before Arthur died in 1949, aged just 48.

distraught because she wasn't there in his final hours. It was the 22nd December, 1949, at about five o'clock in the evening.

Father had suffered from heart problems and angina and in those days, doctors didn't do a lot. They had sent him home with some pills for Christmas. Mother had expected Father to go back into hospital after Christmas but of course, it was too late by then.

It was terribly difficult and very, very sad. Mother took it very badly, she said she didn't feel she could carry on. Then her mother, my grandma, said, 'look, you have got two children – you have to look after them now.' She then summoned all the family together and I remember her saying, 'oh, you will miss your Father.' I always remember that and I replied, 'yes, I will'.

Christmas that year was a very sad time. I remember a very fancy box of crackers that Father wanted to give me as a nice present which I never opened because it was a Christmas present from him. I would imagine we went to my Grandmother's for Christmas Day and I remember going to various of Mother's friends and staying with them for a few days afterwards.

Mother decided she would have to move from Bradwell Hall Farm to something more manageable for my brother who was hoping to come and work on the farm. We decided we would like to buy somewhere and there was also my schooling to think about.

After many months of house-hunting we found a lovely house near Nantwich, Cheshire, called Whitehaven, which had 20 acres of land. My brother Peter found a job at an agricultural engineers in Crewe and also farmed the land at Whitehaven, rearing a few cows, poultry and pigs.

Luckily I had passed my 11-plus entrance examination so was able to transfer from Orme Girls High in Newcastle to Nantwich Grammar School about four miles away – and travelled each morning by taxi! This was a very good school and there I met a girl called Jill Cooper and we have remained friends to this day. Jill and her husband Michael Johnson visit us each year and have done so for the past 50 years!

A few years later, when Peter was only 21, he married Barbara Hegan and moved about two miles up the road to a little cottage called The Laurels leaving Mother and me in the house on our own with a sheepdog called Bess.

It was a struggle for Mother – she couldn't get a widow's pension because there were just a few months between when Father died and this coming into force but we managed and we had a very good accountant who used to come and help her. She had had nothing to do with the accounts as Father used to do everything. But she was hard-working and always had been and she got income from the poultry and the eggs and the milking herd which Peter managed. We managed to carry on farming Whitehaven.

Mother had two brothers who were a great help to her. The one, my Uncle Gerald, the eldest, helped at Whitehaven. All in all, the whole family helped but Mother's face was very sad and she never wanted to marry again. She also had lots of friends who used to take her shopping, and to the WI.

She wanted to drive and tried going round the

fields with my brother but was too nervous so she gave that up. Then of course when I could drive I was able to take her around and that was a big help. The family were amazing.

So we all got by. I have very fond memories of my Father. He was a very caring, very kind person who was so loved and he would talk to anyone. He was loved by all the neighbours and friends – he had lots of friends and used to enjoy going to parties.

A photograph of May and her two brothers, Jim and Gerald, in their Ellesmere College uniform, circa early 1920s.

His death probably made me stronger and more determined. It hits you and then you think, right, I've got to carry on. I haven't got the back-up of a father.

CHAPTER THREE

GROWING UP

I N THE summer of 1950, when I was 12, I went on my first foreign holiday – hiking in Normandy in France with the Girl Guides. It was very exciting. There were eight of us and we would stay in various youth hostels – Nissen huts that the soldiers had used, often sleeping on straw mattresses. It was quite an experience. It was very hot and we used to walk 15 to 20 miles a day along country lanes from one hostel to the next.

Della and her fellow guides would walk 15 to 20 miles a day in summer heat, from one youth hostel to the next.

In those days the lanes were so quiet, you didn't see much traffic and we had to walk from village to village to find the youth hostels. They were very basic. I remember drinking out of bowls because they didn't have cups but the tea tasted wonderful. We would go to the little shop in the village and get milk which was always ladled out of a big bowl and we used to say – what was 'milk'? – *lait*. We learnt a little French along the way!

Della with a freshly-baked baguette on her French hiking holiday.

We didn't have proper walking gear – just lace-up leather shoes which caused a lot of blisters, and heavy rucksacks on our backs. When we reached the youth hostel we would get a meal – usually loads of bread and butter and soup. Of course, French bread is always delicious. To us it was a real treat having fresh bread as Mother didn't make bread at home.

One day, we went on to the beach and noticed these un-exploded mines with spikes in, just left on the sand – all remnants of the war. It was quite a shock. We saw signs of damage from the war. I remember in Rouen going around the cathedral and seeing all these statues

With friend and fellow Guide Christine, in Normandy.

outside with their heads knocked off! I remember that vividly. I don't know how that happened. Perhaps it was something to do with religion.

Wherever we went, people along the roadside were so happy to see us, being English! They would give us lots of things like strawberries. One day, a Frenchman gave us a lift in the back of his little lorry. They were so welcoming because they were relieved the war was

The Moulin Rose café with a windmill on top and a waymarker post in the foreground.

over and that things were beginning to get back to normal again. It was a very good experience although I have never particularly liked walking since!

Della as a teenager. She was by now becoming a talented young cook, winning lots of prizes in cookery competitions.

And aged 15, in a ballgown for brother Peter's 21ˢᵗ birthday.

After passing my GCEs, I was offered a place on a three-year course for a degree in Hotel Management at Radbrook College near Shrewsbury. But Mother would have been left on her own and I felt she needed me so I turned the offer down. Instead, after leaving school I decided to get a job and also to join Nantwich Young Farmers Club.

I went to work at a small restaurant in Nantwich called The Cheshire Cat, run by a manageress called Mrs Whalley who was a good friend of the family. I helped her with the daily running of the restaurant, cooking lots of the puddings.

I enjoyed cooking and at this time entered many cookery competitions at local agricultural shows, in particular the one at Nantwich, coming home with lots of prizes. There was a big entry – mainly farmers' wives. I started entering the competitions when I was still a schoolgirl at Nantwich Grammar School and carried on for several years. I would make various dishes, including lemon curd and sandwich cakes, and puddings like Charlotte Rousse.

There was one competition – three ways of cooking Cheshire cheese, and that's when I won the Woman's Own bronze medal – of course Nantwich was noted for its Cheshire cheese. I made lobster croquettes using cheese, cheese straws and a cheese and onion flan. That's my claim to fame!

Della's treasured certificates from prize-winning entries in Nantwich Show among others, from the late 50s to early 60s.

I decided to move on from The Cheshire Cat after two years and was offered a job at a country club called The Bowmere at Tarporley near Chester, working as a receptionist, also helping with the cooking. I spent two years there.

Lots of the Young Farmers would congregate in Blackpool, around the third week of September, after the corn and hay harvest. While on holiday there, I met a charming young farmer called Tony Brookshaw.

Young Farmers holiday to Blackpool, 1956. Left: John Parkin, Della and the charming young farmer she met there for the first time: Anthony Brookshaw.

Below: Tony and Della on the left, middle row, at Blackpool Ice Rink.

We seemed to get on well and he asked if I went to many Young Farmers dances. We met again at a dance at the Corbet Arms in Market Drayton,

On the way home from their YFC holiday to Blackpool.

Shropshire. This led to us going on lots of outings and holidays together, including to the Isle of Man with our friends John and Wendy Cooper and Richard and Anne Ellwood, who all lived at Wybunbury near Nantwich.

Our subsequent holiday with John and Wendy was touring Spain, in our little Renault Dauphine car. We all ended up marrying our partners. Tony and I got engaged in 1958. I was 19 and Tony was 23.

Tony and I started to look for a farm in which to start our married life together. We visited numerous ones, some with just a few acres and others with larger estates. We were not concerned whether we were going to rent or purchase them.

Father-in-law Stan Brookshaw said to me on day one: 'I want something nice for you, Della, so we will keep looking.'

In 1960, after we had been engaged for two years, he finally found us the ideal farm. One day, after the races at Bangor-on-Dee, Tony told me that his father was interested in buying a farm nearby.

He pointed to a house on a hill and said, 'you see the pile of bricks up there, that's the place we're thinking of buying'. I was worried because I thought it was far too big for us to live in, but I somehow felt we would live there. And that pile of bricks was The Plassey. In June of that year, we negotiated a price and agreed to purchase it from a Mr Harrison, a Shropshire farmer, who had owned it for four years and had put a bailiff – a farm manager – in the wing of The Plassey and his in-laws in the other part.

He never actually lived there himself. He then decided to sell it because he had seen another farm in Wem which he liked better and that's when Tony's father purchased it. It was to become our home until the present day.

The original owner had been Frank Lloyd, a well-known horse auctioneer from Wrexham, who had sold a lot of horses during the war and regularly held auctions in the Wynnstay in Wrexham.

He had spent a lot of money turning The Plassey into a model dairy farm with all the latest equipment. Mr Lloyd was

Frank Lloyd

said to be the illegitimate son of Sir Watkin Williams Wyn which might explain how he had the money to buy the place.

Although it was built as a model dairy farm, by the time we moved in it was very dilapidated – and Mr Harrison hadn't done anything to improve it during his short time there.

We were really looking forward to moving into The Plassey but I could have lost Tony before we even got married in the July of that year.

First of all, in January 1960, Tony had suffered a broken leg while riding one of his father's horses in a race at Warwick. He had to wear a plaster up as far as his thigh. Then, shortly before Tony and I got married, Tony was helping out with the harvest at The Plassey. They were baling hay and he decided to drive the baler even though he had still got his leg in plaster from the riding accident.

At some stage there was a bale of hay in front blocking his way so he had to get off the tractor to move it, and then the tractor with the baler behind started to move! He somehow managed to get on with his leg in plaster but couldn't put the brake on.

Unfortunately it carried on where there was a bit of a slope and he went through a hedge down the slope into a wooded area between trees with the baler still on the back and came to a halt at the bottom. A workman at the time was cutting a hedge and thought, Mr Brookshaw's disappeared! He went over and he was still sitting on the tractor!

Tony said, 'oh I can get back up again,' and

somehow he managed to go back up the slope between the trees. But then he thought, 'that was a bad
idea, I don't think I'll do that any more.'

Fortunately, he hadn't hurt himself but that evening his mother rang up and said to me, 'you nearly
didn't have a husband.' I said, 'oh, what's happened?' And then she told me the story! I'm afraid
Tony didn't really learn from what happened. He
had a good few scary experiences after that. It's a
Brookshaw trait!

CHAPTER FOUR

THE PLASSEY STORY BEGINS

Della – now Mrs Della Brookshaw – cuts her home-made
wedding cake alongside her new husband, Tony.

W E MARRIED on July 23rd, 1960, at St
Mary's Church, Acton near Nantwich. I
had eight bridesmaids and we had the reception for 150 guests at my home with a lovely marquee with a green and yellow striped lining (the
racing colours of the Brookshaws.)

I made and iced a three-tier cake for my own wedding. Tony was not able to kneel in church as he had

still not fully recovered from his broken leg and his plaster was only removed a few days beforehand!

Tony, like other family members, was a keen

Just married: Tony and Della outside St Mary's Church.

amateur jockey, riding many of his father's horses and also ones belonging to friends. He rode mostly at point-to-points but in the run-up to our wedding, would have had the opportunity to ride one of his father's horses, Holly Bank, in the Grand National at Liverpool in March 1960 had it not been for his broken leg.

Instead, his place was offered to his brother Peter but much to the disappointment of all the family, the horse fell at the Chair Jump. Tony continued riding, going hunting with Sir Watkin Williams Wynn's Hunt for many years. Holly Bank was his favourite horse, which eventually retired and ended his days at The Plassey.

At the Wedding Breakfast, from left: Elizabeth, Judy Brookshaw, Bill Windsor, newly-weds Tony and Della, Wendy, Jill Barnes, Della's mother May and brother Peter.

Bridesmaids at Della and Tony's wedding: Susan Cooke (also a niece) now Okell; Tony and Della; Bill Windsor; Wendy Cooper; David Parton; Beryl Latham; Peter Brookshaw; Elizabeth Brassington, now Hughes; standing behind her to the right: Randle Cooke (cousin) and his sister Pat Cooke, became Peake; Jill Brookshaw (niece of Tony); Judy Brookshaw (also a niece).

We had planned a seven-day honeymoon touring the Lake District, but as we were both so excited about starting our new life together at The Plassey, we decided to travel back home a couple of days earlier. This upset our friends' plans to play tricks on us as they weren't expecting us back so soon.

So they quickly decorated the farm with lots of 'welcome home' signs, and placed crow scarers in the trees below our bedroom window!

We started out with a herd of 60 dairy cows and

Della, following her return from honeymoon. On the right is Jill Brookshaw, Tony's niece (subsequently Jill Barnes).

Tony only employed one man and a young lad to help. Tony was always out of the house at 5.30am ready to milk the cows. It was a seven-day working week in those days. Breakfast was 8.30am, lunch at 1pm and tea at 5.30pm. We managed to stick to these times as Tony's mother had always been very strict with timekeeping when he lived at home.

We ran the farm in partnership for seven years with Tony's parents who farmed at Aychley Farm near Market Drayton, and shared agricultural machinery and workmen who came and helped with the harvest. It was my job to supply them with lots of tea and orangeade and also their cooked lunch during haymaking and corn harvests.

Plassey House has about 25 rooms with a wing adjoining which was used for cheesemaking and staff accommodation. In 1961 after about 12 months' residence in the large house, we decided to make use of the empty rooms and apply for planning permission to convert the old cheesemaking rooms into a flat which is now called the Bottom Flat. This was rented out to my brother's wife's parents for 12 months. We continued to rent this flat out and found it was a great way of keeping the empty rooms dry and also helped by providing us with extra income.

I remained a keen cook and I had a big kitchen and pantry at The Plassey which I filled with jars of

Della using her trusty Esse cooking range in one of the photographs taken of her by Ideal Home magazine.

chutneys and pickles. I didn't know it at the time but it was to feature in an article in Ideal Home magazine!

Three of them came up from London to interview me. It was originally thanks to a tip-off from my friend Jill. The magazine wanted to do an article about somebody from Wales who was good at cooking and she said, 'oh, I have got a friend in Wales who is good at cooking,' and they got in touch and came up and did the interview and took photographs.

Della talks to a reporter from Ideal Home magazine.

I had made a lemon meringue pie and a Charlotte Rousse to show them what I could do, and took what I had cooked into the pantry. The female reporter followed me and spotted all these jams and chutneys and she couldn't believe it. She said, 'oh my goodness, I have never seen anything like this.' So they said, 'scrap those two hours of work, we'll focus on the jams and chutneys'. In London they had never seen anything like it, even then in the early 1960s.

The reporter was so impressed with Della's chutneys, pickles and jams, she made them the focus of her article.

People didn't bottle fruit in London – they hadn't got the fruit we had in the gardens and in the orchard, like the damsons and the pears. It all came from produce grown here. I don't bottle fruit any more because we've now got big freezers but in those days bottling was the method used to preserve.

So they concentrated on all my jams, jellies and chutneys lining the shelves of the pantry. There was lemon curd, pickled pears, pickled damsons, gooseberries – all out of our own orchards. Some of those jars of damsons dating back to the 1960s are in the kitchen at the National Trust stately home of Erddig now! Several friends and relations saw the article and were impressed! One or two said they had tried the recipes.

Cooking has always been very important to me. I learned a lot from my Mother and also at school – it was called Domestic Science then. Everything was basic but very good – I had a very good teacher at the grammar school. I enjoyed cooking and Mother always encouraged me.

The finished article: a double-page spread on Della and her love of 'bottling and preserving' – with recommended recipes.

CHAPTER FIVE

BECOMING PARENTS

AFTER moving in at The Plassey, I was keen to get know people in the area and our friend and neighbour Sheila Lewis introduced me to Erbistock WI, which I remained a member of for nearly 50 years until it sadly disbanded in 2018.

It had started in 1927 and grew to about 25 members, meeting on the second Thursday of each month. The meetings were held in a small wooden building on the outskirts of the village of Erbistock. At the start, one of the members would play the piano and we all stood up to sing Jerusalem, (the WI's anthem). The WI movement had begun at Stoney Creek, Ontario, in Canada in 1897 with the aim to encourage women of rural communities to meet up together.

As the old building was getting very dilapidated, we decided to move our meetings to a redundant village school in Erbistock. Lots of interesting outings were arranged, visiting numerous stately homes and special exhibitions. We also entertained other WIs with special evenings and trips. The WIs were renowned for their cooking skills and many cookery competitions were arranged during the year.

There was quite a lot of rivalry among other Women's Institutes – each wanting to take home the first prize! We celebrated our 90th anniversary in 2017 with a party in the village hall. But by then, the village hall was only getting used by ourselves and our membership had dwindled to just eight. We had to disband, much to the disappointment of us all, after 50 years of being a member myself.

Erbistock WI winning first prize at Ellesmere.
From left: Dorothy Blake, Elsie Evans, Janet Owens, Muriel Morris, Della, Brookshaw and Sheila Lewis.

On July 3rd, 1962, two years after we married, our eldest daughter Julie Mary was born in Wrexham Maelor Hospital. It was a difficult birth as she was a breech baby – born naturally. These days it would have been a Caesarean section but back then, there were very few Caesareans carried out. She weighed 8lb 6oz, which was considered quite a large baby.

Tony was so pleased to have a baby daughter and he sent five dozen pink carnations! The hospital had a job finding enough vases!

I remember taking her for a walk in her pram to introduce ourselves to some new neighbours who had gone to live at a large house situated at the bottom of our drive. This resulted in meeting a little boy called Nicholas who was the same age as Julie.

Julie as a baby.

It was the start of a friendship which continued for many years – they would go to the Convent School in Wrexham together and Nicholas would visit us here at The Plassey and he would play with our children together in the old farm buildings.

It was on New Year's Eve of the year Julie was born, that we decided to host a New Year's Eve Party for all our friends. We cleaned up the rooms in the wing of The Plassey and had the idea of holding the party in the old Tower flat – in the billiard room. It was a very big room with a spiral staircase going from it.

We thought it would be a wonderful place to have a party, so we invited our friends from my area in Nantwich and Tony's in Shropshire and the local neighbours. There were about 80 of us in total. We booked an entertainer to come and play some music, a friend of ours from Nantwich.

Then, about a day beforehand, a warning was issued about a terrific cold spell coming with sub-zero temperatures. But we decided it was too late to cancel the party, we would carry on. I remember the phone going on the day itself and this friend asked, 'have you got much snow yet?' I said, 'no we haven't, but it's beginning to sleet a bit.'

All I was worried about was that he wasn't going to come but he said, 'oh yes, we're still coming, we just wondered what it was like.' So I said, 'at the moment it's fine.'

We did all the catering ourselves, and Grandmother Brookshaw got a friend to help with the meats and bring a ham. I did all the puddings and we arranged to have the food in one of the big bedrooms upstairs.

And we put up a big Christmas tree – using the top of a fir tree that had fallen. We took it upstairs and put it in the corner by the spiral staircase and decorated it. It looked very pretty and festive and we lit the fire in the billiard room and put electric fires and paraffin heaters everywhere because there was no central heating of course, and it was getting very cold.

The temperatures continued to fall and we began to get worried that people wouldn't arrive, but anyway everybody came, all 80, including our entertainer – despite the grim weather warnings!

We served our guests a special cocktail which they used to have at hunt meetings made of Cointreau,

vodka and lemonade which we mixed in a huge
bowl and ladled into glasses. It was very potent anyway and then my uncle – my mother's brother – spotted a bottle of gin on the side and emptied that in as
well! They all loved it.

We had games where we would dress up – the
men as ladies in dresses and the women as men with
trousers and bow ties. We played musical chairs and
had dances and lots of fun. I remember one of the
men carrying one of the ladies, putting her in the
bath and switching the water on! We had lots of fun
that night – it was just a lovely way of seeing in the
New Year. Everybody was in a wonderful mood –
we never forgot that party for years.

Meanwhile, it had started to snow steadily. Fortunately, most of our friends were farmers and had
come in Land Rovers equipped with a shovel in the
back as farmers would in those days. I remember
them heading home, probably at about two or three
in the morning, with the snow already several inches
deep and drifting. But they got home all right anyway and of course, back then, there were no drink-
drive laws!

It was a very cold night – we didn't know it at the
time but it was to be the start of one of the harshest
cold spells on record. Despite the falling temperatures, we managed to keep all our guests reasonably
warm, and it turned out a great success.

The New Year marked the start of the really severe
wintry weather. As I was taking the decorations

down the snow was getting worse and worse and the temperature kept falling. That's when we had all these bursts. From then on we just had to buckle down and make the best of it.

The Denbigh to St Asaph bus struggles along icy roads in February 1963, during one of the coldest winters on record.

It was very tough – all the cattle were inside the shippon and we had to carry water and food to them. It was quite difficult for the milk lorry to come and collect our milk. In the end we had to take the milk churns to the bottom of the drive with a tractor and trailer. The postwoman had to walk up the drive because she couldn't cycle. A lot of the pipes supplying us with water had all frozen. Tony was kept busy carrying buckets of water to supply the cattle.

The house was also very cold as the only heating we had was the Esse cooker, coal fires and electric heaters. I remember lots of heaters being used to thaw pipes out and the pipes then bursting.

We had a tremendous burst in the top flat – the cylinder collapsed. I think it was because we had left the immersion heater on. The water in the pipes had frozen and the cylinder collapsed inwardly. I remember going into the hallway to the back staircase and seeing water cascading down the stairs.

After recovering from months of freezing temperatures and repairing the many frozen pipes, we decided to continue renovating disused farm buildings. And in 1964, a widowed aunt of mine, May Gibson, wanted to come to live here at The Plassey. She helped us renovate the top flat for her to move here from the village of Mobberley in Cheshire. A lot of the furniture here once belonged to her. She had a very interesting life – her second husband had been a doctor, and he would go off on trips to China and Japan and bring back exotic presents for her.

May had a son called Roy who was quite a delicate child. He suffered from muscular dystrophy, I can remember him in a wheelchair, he was only about 44 when he died.

When she lived with us, May had a little grey Austin 10 that she used to drive. She used to beep the horn outside the house because she liked me to go with her on shopping trips. I remember being so busy and this horn would be going 'beep beep beep'.

She used to tear round the corner in Marchwiel opposite the church and never stop at the Stop sign! Tony thought of her as a 'difficult one who liked to have her own way.' She was a real character – I just wish I had asked her so much more about her life when I had the chance.

May was quite a formidable person and very clever. After living at The Plassey for about two years, she suddenly decided she wanted to build a house of her own, which she did. She was already in her 80s by then but she went on to be 100. She moved to a nursing home in the end but only for about the last two to three years. I always remember them saying in the home that she was a real lady.

May's first husband was a Mr Charles Lutwyche, a very wealthy man whose family owned Lutwyche Hall in Much Wenlock, Shropshire.

May with her first husband, Mr Charles Lutwyche.

They held their wedding reception at the Salamanca Hotel in Wrenbury, Cheshire, which was owned by her parents.

Della's Aunt May on her wedding day, circa 1913, to Charles Lutwyche, outside the Salamanca Hotel, Wrenbury, owned by her parents. Della's mother, also May, can be seen as a young child to the right of the front wheel of Mr Lutwyche's car.

The car in the photographs was the first one to be seen in Wrenbury village. My mother was a bridesmaid, you can see her in the photograph standing just to the right of the front wheel of the car. She was born in 1908 and would have been about five at the time. Unfortunately, Charles Lutwyche spent a lot of his money on drink and became an alcoholic and died young as a result.

One morning, about 30 to 40 years ago, I went to the Co-op and on the counter was a newspaper with a headline which caught my eye: 'Great fire at hall'. It was Lutwyche Hall. I have always intended to go back and see if it's still standing. It was such a coincidence to go to the shop that day and see that paper.

Our next tenants were what we called the bachelors. First of all, a nice young man called Sid. He was followed by another bachelor called 'John the Biscuit' (because he worked as a rep for a biscuit firm!) He occupied the Bottom Flat.

Next came Kevin who took the Top Flat. We now had three single men who had great times together. Our new tenants were very nice. They helped us with the hay harvest and really enjoyed themselves. We often see Sid who is now married and living in Stafford. He says he has 'dined on' his many experiences here at The Plassey and recalls the many happy times he spent here.

One year we went on holiday to Abersoch and left them in charge. We had bullocks in the shippon at the time – the bachelors used to go in to make sure everything was all right. One night a bullock jumped straight over a high wall – frightening them to death!

In our early years at The Plassey, I bought some day-old chicks and reared them in one of the haylofts which is now the staffroom at the hairdressers. Then we had the idea of converting the loft floor for laying hens. We put raised slats about two feet up and some laying boxes to collect the eggs. We kept hens for a number of years and had lots of eggs. I enjoyed keeping them and had about 100 at one point. I used to sell the eggs to a company which would buy them from me.

I then decided I wanted to rear some turkeys for Christmas. I had some 30-day-old birds which I reared in a loose-box (an enclosed stall in which we used to keep heifers) in front of the building which is now an ice cream parlour. I think they were Norfolk Bronze. At Christmas I took them to the auction in Wrexham and sold them. I kept about four which I dressed myself for friends and family. We had one on Christmas Day.

I was expecting one of the children at the time, I think it was 1963 when my second daughter, Jane, was on the way. The trouble was, I didn't enjoy eating my own turkeys. I got sentimentally attached to them! I also had about six Muscovy ducks and another four or five which I reared. But in the end they got so tame that they would follow me to the back door of the house and make a mess so we had to get rid of them!

It was around this time that I decided I might like to ride a horse. With Tony being such a good rider, I decided one day to ask him if he would teach me to ride, because I was quite keen to perhaps join in hunting and we had these two horses in the farm stables – one was a point-to-point race horse and the other was for hunting. He said I could have a go and told me to jump on the race horse. It was a fit young horse and not suitable for teaching somebody on.

He put me on and said, 'off you go!'. It took off with me and frightened me to death! I never did it again. And Tony just said, 'oh, you'll never ride'. He hadn't any patience to teach me!

A watercolour of Lutwyche Hall painted in 1887. The fire in 1989 gutted the east wing, but the Hall exists to this day.

CHAPTER SIX

A NEW DIRECTION

JANE LOUISE was the next baby to be born, in August 1964 – two years after her sister, and also at Wrexham Maelor Hospital. She was christened at Bangor-on-Dee church and for godparents we chose Mrs Margaret Byrd, Mrs Ann Furnival and Mr Bill Windsor.

We enjoyed having the two girls and a neighbour called Joanne had a little boy, Nicholas, who became a good friend for them and joined them when they all went to the Convent School in Wrexham.

Julie, on the right, with her younger sister, Jane.

We were also lucky to have some more playmates for the girls when a family by the name of Owen bought a neighbouring house called Eyton Grange, only a mile away. There were two girls around the same age, Claire and Karen, who became good friends of Julie and Jane. They all had ponies and rode together for many years. Lots of happy times were spent here at The Plassey over the years with them all attending the local school at Marchwiel and then Penley School.

Julie on a tricycle, with Jane at The Plassey.

In those days, I used to enjoy going to the sale rooms at Overton – I was always interested in furniture and antiques and Wingetts auctioneers used to organise a sale each month at the Bryn-y-Pys sale room. I wanted to fill The Plassey with nice pieces of furniture and I always enjoyed going over to have a look what was available.

I found lots of interesting bits and pieces and one day I bought some dining chairs. After I paid for them, I was standing by a lady and mentioned that I'd bought the chairs but didn't know how I was going to get them home. She told me she lived at Marchwiel and asked me where I lived and then offered to drop them off for me.

After we chatted it turned out that she had two children the same age as ours who both attended the same school as our two – Marchwiel School.

This person was Carol Jenkins who became a friend and still is, after all these years. Carol and I used to meet at the sale rooms and she would buy bits and pieces as well. We have always had a love for antiques. She was friendly with another mother, Anne Hamlett, whose children also went there.

We all became friends together and now they are both in their 80s like me and we have been friends all these years – and it all came about through going to the sale room.

Della with friends Anne Hamlett
and Carol Jenkins, many years later.

In 1967, we decided to convert the old-fashioned shippon and build a new herringbone milking parlour. The problem was that although they were beautiful buildings, they were out of date and had to be modernised. Tony set about digging out a pit in part of the shippon to accommodate the parlour. Unfortunately, something unexpected was to happen which changed everything for good.

A disease called Foot and Mouth arrived in the UK shortly after Tony started to dig the pit. No-one was allowed to move any cattle, and work on the new parlour had to stop due to restrictions on people coming and going at the farm. Workmen weren't allowed to come and do any building work. This put a lot of strain on Tony, having to milk 70 cows in the outdated shippon.

This was a very sad and stressful time for us all, wondering who would be the next victim of this dreaded disease. It came steadily closer until we heard that there was Foot and Mouth in the area.

I think it was Oswestry where it started around here. One day, I decided to climb up the spiral staircase to view the many fires burning in the neighbourhood and I noticed seven diggers at work. The carcasses of infected cattle had been piled up in deep pits and set on fire. It might actually have made the situation worse – from the crows eating them and the infection being blown in the wind.

The whole herd had to be slaughtered whether they had the disease or not, really healthy cattle and calves, it was so upsetting. People living at infected farms weren't allowed to leave, they had to stay put and have everything delivered – a bit like Covid. We were fortunate that we didn't have that traumatic experience.

A policeman oversees precautions against Foot and Mouth Disease in October 1967 at Oswestry Cattle Market.

You had to be wary wherever you went, especially visiting other farms because of the risk of transmitting the infection. But I remember Father Brookshaw at Aychley coming over – we were still in partnership with him then – and he would visit regularly. Tony was putting straw at the bottom of the drive with disinfectant on it. He said, 'that's a waste of time,' and he was quite right because in the end they found that Foot and Mouth was transmitted through birds and the wind.

Foot and Mouth went on for about five months. Fortunately, we did escape but nonetheless it changed our lives as we decided to sell our herd altogether to a victim of the disease and look for alternative sources of income.

This decision came about after a conversation with local seedsman Sid Edwards. He used to come every month for orders to sell corn for the cattle. He remarked that he had a customer who had been a victim of Foot and Mouth and was looking for a herd of cows. Tony and I talked about it and we thought, what about selling our herd to him?

We got in touch and told him we might be interested. We had a word with my father-in-law to see what he thought and he said that it could be a good idea, as our buildings were outdated and badly needed modernising. So we put the whole herd of 70 cows out to tender and this farmer, who had lost his entire stock because of Foot and Mouth, bought them all.

Selling up was a very big decision but we had got the farm cottages and knew that we had to make use of them to bring in money. The buildings were essentially redundant because they all revolved around the cows and calves. We decided to let the cottages – we'd had a farmworker living in one – but the others were derelict so we needed to do them up first.

In the main house, we made two more flats out of the redundant wing which used to be for dairy and cheese-making and accommodation for the maids. They were all empty rooms as was the Tower flat.

Our friends couldn't understand why we wanted strangers to come and live so close by. They would say, you don't want people living in a part of your own house! But we didn't mind because otherwise it would have got damp and we enjoyed people being around.

One of our early tenants was a gentleman on the Agricultural Advisory Committee (ADAS) and he was the one who first suggested we have caravans. He and his wife were members of the Camping Club and thought The Plassey would be great for holding camping rallies. We took their advice and went on to host rallies from various different clubs for several years and began to take caravanners.

Rallies of all sorts became a regular feature at The Plassey.

Meanwhile, we decided to keep sheep instead of cattle. The land at The Plassey is very heavy and clayey and never been that suitable for dairy cattle but is very good for grazing sheep which eat the grass and keep it down.

Tony bought some very good sheep – he used to take them to the market at Ellesmere where they had a competition for the best lambs and would often come back with first prize. But it was a lot of work. People think sheep farming is easy but it is ongoing and lambing especially was very hard work during bad weather – usually in about January. We hadn't really got very good buildings for rearing sheep and for lambing.

Nowadays, farms have very good facilities with special pens but we didn't have all that.

And of course, every year, you have to shear the sheep. We had about 100 and two men used to come to shear them, Ogwyn Jones and Elwyn Davies from Betws-y-Coed.

They would arrive early in the morning and I would give them a cup of tea or orange juice and then lunch in the house. They usually had a hot meal and it always ended up with trifle. And they used to complain that I would give them too much to eat because they couldn't bend very well afterwards!

They would end up at the Fox and Hounds just up the road, drinking until late evening and then return to Betws-y-Coed in their little van full of all their shearing equipment. How they managed to drive home afterwards, I don't know!

Eventually, we sold our sheep and the men brought their own from Betws-y-Coed to graze the land. They used to sell the wool which in those days was worth quite a lot but in later years, demand for wool fell and it didn't really pay to shear them, but of course sheep have to be sheared anyway.

Elwyn visited us a couple of years ago. He'd brought a caravan and was staying at The Plassey and he reminisced about all the fun they used to have!

As we were getting more popular with holiday-makers, we decided to apply for planning permission to be allowed to keep more caravans but unfortunately the local council turned this down at the time, claiming it would be an eyesore in the district and that the entrance was too dangerous.

CHAPTER SEVEN

THE PLASSEY TAKES SHAPE

ON OCTOBER 20th, 1970, our son John Stanley was born at Wrexham Maelor Hospital. We had a great celebration and Tony was so pleased to have a son as well as two daughters, that he hung a blue sheet over the front door!

John Brookshaw as a toddler.

This was the same year that Tony decided to build a swimming pool for the family. I was sceptical at first. I said, 'you can't have an outdoor pool in this climate in Wales,' and he said, 'no, it will have a roof.' I said it would be really expensive, but he insisted that it wouldn't be.

We built the pool where there had been old stallion stables. This was an excellent area as the stables were redundant. There were four stables where they used to have the stallions, with a yard that they could exercise in. We had to knock all that down but we retained the stables in the building and those are now the changing rooms and some of the mangers are still inside them.

Tony did most of the work himself with the help of a farm labourer. He shored it up with old railway sleepers and lined it with a blue plastic liner to hold the water. This has been replaced over the years with blue tiles. The swimming pool now has toilet and shower facilities and changing rooms. In fact, it *is* expensive to run but has proved a big success.

Tony, hard at work digging the new swimming pool in 1970.

The pool was originally intended to be solely for the family but over time, we decided to let the cara-vanners use it for free as part of their fees. We keep it going all year round with the temperature at about 80 degrees.

In 1972, our friend and neighbour Bernard Owens introduced Tony to Wrexham Lions Club, which had about 30 members. This is an international organisation whose aim is to help people in need. In the years from 1973 to 1979, we hosted six pony shows and gymkhana events for the Lions, with the proceeds going to local charities.

They were held on the front field at The Plassey. We also had vintage machinery shows which were a two-day event. One year the famous Fred Dibnah brought along his own steam engine. Tony was elected Lions president in around 1976. This meant a lot of extra work such as arranging dances, meetings, visiting other Lions Clubs and lots more. This often involved myself and I found it very enjoyable meeting lots of people, all from different walks of life.

By 1973, Julie and Jane were already confident riders. Jane is on the white pony, Silver, and Julie is on Tosca.

A pony gymkhana in August 1974, at The Plassey. From left Della's mother, May, Della with son John; daughter Jane riding Silver and friend Karen Owens on horseback.

The Lions Club used some of our barns to hold dances and had various themes such as Dallas Night, Hawaii Night, and The Night The Ship Went Down!. These were all fancy-dress occasions and proved very popular. Other charity events called 'Vino Beanos' were held at Lindisfarne College – a very large hall near the village of Ruabon. The Lions Club ladies provided the food and the men were in charge of the barbecue.

Della and Tony taking part in The Night The Ship Went Down!

On one very cold, frosty occasion we thought we would try lighting a fire in the large fireplace in the Main Hall. Unfortunately, a fire had not been lit for many years and the chimney was cold and damp and didn't draw properly. As a result, huge clouds of smoke billowed into the room instead of going up the chimney. As the place filled up with smoke, most of the guests unfortunately left!

The Lions 18th Charter Anniversary Dinner at Bryn Howel Hotel, on Friday, October 24th, 1980. Lions President Tony Brookshaw and Della are pictured with Wrexham Mayor John Thomas and his wife.

The barns at The Plassey were also used many times to raise funds for the local church at Bangor-on-Dee. Christmas was always a special time for the Lions and they all took turns in driving the Father Christmas float which went around the nearby

Some of the programme
cards from the many Lions
events held at The Plassey
over the years.

towns and villages collecting funds for local charities. Guy Fawkes Night on November 5th was also an
important evening for the club as members were in
charge of organising Wrexham Bonfire and Fireworks Display in the central park in Wrexham. The
men were responsible for lighting the fireworks,
which was always a worrying time!

Wrexham Council would build the bonfire, which
was a great help, and the Lions ladies supplied all
the hotdogs and toffee apples. It was always a very
hectic night making about one thousand hotdogs!

We continued with rallies at The Plassey through
the 1970s and applied for planning permission again
in 1977 for 20 caravans. After a few months, permission was finally agreed and we went ahead with taking fewer rallies and eventually stopped them
altogether to focus on looking after the

holidaymakers. Over the following few months, we converted some redundant farm buildings into toilets and a campsite shop for the caravanners to have their daily newspapers, milk and bread etc. In 1978 we decided to build a clubhouse for them, so they had somewhere to congregate with their families and enjoy a few drinks together.

We built it overlooking the caravan field which had a good view over the park. We raised it to first floor level with an outside balcony. The clubhouse

Tony on a quadbike appearing to be rounding up sheep, helped by son John, amidst the caravans.

The caravan site at The Plassey starts to take shape.

was designed in a similar style to the famous 'Treetops' in Kenya so that's what we called it! Underneath, we installed toilet and shower facilities and also a sauna.

From this point on, everything just evolved, with one thing leading to another.

The caravanners loved the new clubhouse and lots of people offered to help run it. We had three couples from Liverpool who came every weekend to run the bar voluntarily. They just loved being at The Plassey, they always said 'they were coming home.'

In 1979 we decided to alter the main house and live at the front where there are lovely views. The house was very cold at the time, with the only heating from our Esse cooker and coal fires, so we installed central heating and built a new kitchen in one of the front rooms.

When we were deciding what to use our old kitchen for, a young student arrived in a bright yellow sports car called Rosie. She was doing teacher-training at the local Cartrefle College and looking for accommodation so with her help we converted the redundant rooms into a flat. It was the 1970s 'Flower Power' era and she would often walk around with bare feet, much to our amusement!

Rosie used to come and help with our children, especially Jane, teaching her to paint and draw. She was great. She was very keen on art and Jane used to go to her flat at night and paint with her and make all sorts of collages. Jane would also go to the hay loft and make creative pieces of art with various bits of cast iron and other materials – I would go up there and find them all on display!

Rosie in the paddling pool with Julie and Jane, and fellow tenants John and Sid and sheepdog Roy.

Rosie stayed with us for about three years and we enjoyed her company. To the present day we have kept in touch with her – she lives in Spain now. We had great times with all our many tenants and they fitted in well with each other. They became part of the family really.

And of course, Jane went on to excel at Art. After leaving the Maelor School, Penley, Jane took an Art Foundation course at Wrexham's Cartrefle College. It led on to her being accepted at Loughborough College for a three-year degree course.

However, after a term, she decided the course was not to her liking and transferred to Crewe and Alsager College where she obtained a BA in Combined Crafts, winning many awards.

It was around this time that Tony decided he wanted to have flying lessons in a microlight. Eventually he purchased one, an Eagle microlight, and took to the skies – worrying me to death! One day he called at the neighbours' for a coffee – he amazed them by landing in their field.

In those days they didn't have licences, but after so many accidents, they had to. In the end Tony decided it was rather dangerous and after two or three years, gave it up. Thank goodness!

Tony on a field at The Plassey, preparing for take-off.

And taking a bird's eye view of The Plassey caravan site.

I mentioned earlier that Carol Jenkins had become a good friend of mine back in the 1960s after bumping into her at the sale rooms in Overton.

Carol is the mother of Nick Jenkins, the famous TV Dragon from Dragon's Den and creator of the Moonpig gift card company. Long before he became rich and famous, Nick and his older sister Alison would come with their mother to play at The Plassey. Carol used to enjoy taking the children off camping and into the hills of Wales for a few days.

Being a boy, Nick was always the odd one out and he always wanted to do more boisterous things. One day they went for a picnic. Nick was annoying the others so to get rid of him they said to him, 'oh Nick, for goodness sake, go off in the woods and find a snake or something,' thinking it was an impossible task and they would have some peace for a bit. But a few hours later he actually came back with a snake – a grass snake – they couldn't believe it!

Nick was always determined to rise to any challenge but would often end up getting into some predicament. We used to take him fishing and invariably he would get his line tangled up with the branches of the trees.

There was a time, when Nick was about 12, he went off with our son John while we were chatting in the house. They decided to have a ride on Tony's ATV (all-terrain vehicle) and Nick thought he would have a go in the driver's seat.

It was only a three-wheeler and quite difficult to turn. There were some caravans stored in the yard and Nick couldn't turn it properly and he scraped it along one of them!

John and Nick came back into the house and we were all sitting chatting and I can see them now, they both stood at the back of the settee. We said, 'are you

Nick Jenkins

all right', and John said, 'we've had a problem. Nick's scratched a caravan.' His mother was quite annoyed, she said, 'Nicholas, what were you doing?'

He explained that he couldn't turn the bike in time and of course, it wasn't our caravan! I can't remember what exactly happened then, but I recall Carol bringing me a jug as a present and feeling very guilty!

We didn't realise at the time, of course, that he was going to turn out to be such a success but he would always turn his hand to different things and keep going, even if they didn't work out. Jane says of Nick that successful people like him are those who will always have a go, even if at first they fail.

CHAPTER EIGHT

STORMY TIMES

OUR next project was renovating the many derelict farm buildings. In 1984 we changed the old coach-house building into a two-bedroom residence with the intention of letting it out on a yearly short-term let. Everything was progressing well at The Plassey but the following year we suffered a setback – thanks to Mother Nature.

In early June 1985, a freak storm erupted wrecking everything in its path. The sky went completely dark and then a violent hailstorm began which caused a great deal of damage at The Plassey. Huge hailstones thumped down, making lots of dents in the roofs of caravans and cars and covering them with leaves and debris. They also smashed the roof of the swimming pool.

There were actually swimmers in the pool at the time. My mother was in charge and luckily managed to get them into the changing rooms just in time before the whole roof collapsed. It was corrugated plastic and it just shattered, leaving the water covered in plastic sheeting.

The hailstones, which were about two inches across, also damaged all the crops. We were just about to advertise some grass for sale to be cut for hay. But it was flattened and soaked and as a result, we couldn't sell it.

The storm spanned less than five miles – Johnstown village is five miles away and they didn't get it. It lasted for about quarter of an hour then within half an hour, returned for another ten minutes and did more damage. I can remember John running out to collect some of the hailstones. He put a chair on top of his head because they were so fierce.

The storm destroyed the swimming pool roof.

It was a busy time, at the height of the season and in all, about 50 caravans and cars were damaged. It must have cost thousands of pounds to repair but luckily most of the holidaymakers were insured. It was quite a frightening experience for everyone including the livestock – I remember the sheep making such a noise. We've never had anything like that before or since.

Afterwards we just carried on but there was more trouble to come soon after. Tony suffered a nasty accident with a ride-on grass cutter, putting him in hospital for weeks.

Towards the end of the day in question I was cleaning the swimming pool when I heard a shout that someone had been hurt on the caravan park and would I go and help. I ran outside and realised that it was Tony who had been hurt. I saw him on the arms of a man looking very white and shaken.

I said, 'oh it's you, what's happened?' He said, 'it was the lawnmower.'

He had been mowing a slope of the golf course on the ride-on mower and it turned over and caught his heel. We jumped in the car, not thinking to ring for an ambulance. I asked the man who carried him to come with me because I was frightened that I might faint. We shot off to A&E.

They took him straight in and asked what had happened and after examining him, said to my horror, 'have you got the heel?' I said '*what*?' His heel had been sliced off. I think I did nearly faint at that stage. Of course, he had to stay in and then these two men, who would help run the bar, turned up at the hospital and asked if they could do anything.

They agreed to take the gentleman home who had kindly come with me and take over the bar that evening. Eventually I went home later that night, leaving Tony in the hospital where he had to stay for nearly two months.

He had to have a skin graft which involved attaching his damaged heel to his other leg, so I had to make some special pants to put on him that tied on the sides. I used to go every night to see him – at around nine o'clock after I'd finished all the work. Luckily I had lots of helpers including the family.

When he was allowed to come home we managed to rig up a bed downstairs with a pulley to hoist him up – in those days they didn't provide one. I slept in the hall on a mattress because I wanted to be near him.

Unfortunately, matters took a turn for the worse. Tony had been home a couple of days when he complained of pain in his chest. He was a bit short of breath and thought he had pulled a muscle raising himself up on the pulley. In fact, it turned out to be far more serious.

Every morning a surgeon who lived in Overton, a Scottish man called Angus Jameson, would call in on his way to hospital. But on this particular day he was late, he didn't come until about lunchtime.

I went to the door and said, 'Tony's not been very well this morning, he's pulled a muscle or something.' He took a look at him, did a few tests and said, 'I'm just going to the car.' He disappeared and came back and said, 'the ambulance will be here in a minute.'

I had no idea what was happening. The surgeon

kept watching Tony and then the ambulance arrived with its bell ringing and I realised it must be an emergency. They wheeled him out and told me to bring his clothes because he would be staying in.

I followed by car and when I got to the hospital, Dr Cliff Sissons, a consultant cardiologist, was standing at the door of the room where Tony was being treated. He said he needed to talk to me. It sounded serious. He said: 'Tony's had a slight pulmonary embolism and we're waiting for a heparin machine to come from another hospital and dissolve the clot.'

They hadn't told me that this could happen, because of him being immobile. A clot of this kind could be fatal, so it was a big shock.

Tony's Angels: Della (right) and Jane prepare to take part in the Great Erbistock Raft Race on the River Dee, referencing Tony's accident, to raise money for charity.

The surgeon's wife was the anaesthetist and she admitted to me not so long ago that Tony was one of the most worrying patients she'd ever had. They hadn't been able to give him the full anaesthetic as they needed to keep him semi-conscious.

As they attended to separating his legs, she said, 'I do not know how he stood the pain.' We didn't know it at the time but Cliff and his wife Dianne were to become good friends right to the present day.

Despite everything, on July 23rd that year, Tony and I celebrated our Silver Wedding at Bryn Howel Hotel, Llangollen, with about 150 guests. Tony had not long come out of hospital and had to attend in a wheelchair. But he managed the evening really bravely, although he was still in much pain. I kept saying we should put it off but he insisted that he

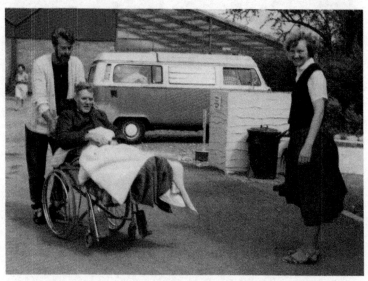

Friend Bert de Jongh, over from Holland with wife Tina for the Silver Wedding Anniversary, pushes Tony's wheelchair.

Despite being in great pain, Tony was determined not to miss the Silver Wedding Anniversary party on July 23rd, 1985.

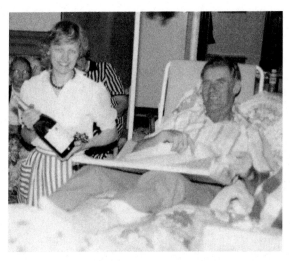

Tony and Della prepare to toast their milestone wedding anniversary with a glass of champagne.

wanted to go. It was that Brookshaw determination!

I had some friends from London staying with me at the time, Jill and Mike, who took him in the car and brought him home just after the meal. We had a Caribbean band organised and a proper dinner and

Tony did manage it although he was in a lot of pain. The surgeon and his wife the anaesthetist came as well – we invited them partly so that if anything went wrong they were there!

Cliff Sissons looked after Tony at Wrexham's War Memorial Hospital and Dianne nursed him all the time. A while later, Tony and I went to a function at a charity dance and Cliff and Di were there. We got chatting, recalling his time in hospital and Tony mentioned having a golf course and Cliff said, 'oh that's interesting, I might come and play one day'.

It was back to the Bryn Howell Hotel, Llangollen, a week later for Jane's 21st birthday. Next to Jane is her grandmother May, father Tony still smiling despite his injury, and Della.

Tony replied, 'come any time you like,' and that's how the friendship started.

It was a very big task to keep things going at The Plassey. It was a lot of work but we got through it and everybody was very helpful – it was like one big happy family there really.

And amidst it all, we celebrated another milestone on August 1st that year – our daughter Jane's 21st birthday which was also held at Bryn Howell Hotel, with 50 guests. It took about six months for Tony to recover fully.

Jane with her siblings Julie and John on her 21st.

CHAPTER NINE

FROM COW SHED TO RESTAURANT

TOWARDS the end of the year, Tony was approached by a brewer, Alan Beresford, who had retired from Border Breweries in Wrexham. He wished to open a small 'real ale' brewery and was interested in setting it up at The Plassey.

We had an area adjoining the restaurant which was a suitable place for a brewery. Tony and Alan went into partnership and opened The Plassey Brewery in October 1985.

This has been very successful and now produces

An early photograph of the fledgling Plassey Brewery.

Tony with brewer Alan Beresford holding a photo board advertising The Plassey's very own beer.

cask-conditioned ales. Later on the brewery moved to larger premises in The Plassey Barn. Ian Dale, a brewer from Wrexham Lager, took it over from Alan, who sadly died in 1989. Since 2017, the brewery has been run by Richard Lever.

Tony and Della toast their new brewery with a glass of ale.

The following year we embarked upon another big project. The old shippon had long been redundant following our momentous decision two decades earlier to sell our dairy herd.

I wanted to turn it into a restaurant, but to preserve this unique building intact with all the cow stalls, glazed brick walls and parquet floors. Tony was not too impressed with this idea. He said it was not intended for people to eat in – it was built for milking cows! He couldn't understand that people would want to go and eat in there. But I had always been interested in having a restaurant, it was one of my ambitions, and was really keen to go ahead.

The shippon cow shed had been redundant for years until its conversion in 1986.

Consequently we applied for planning permission to turn it into a 60-seater restaurant, with a large kitchen, office and toilets and were successful. And of course, we kept the name, so the old shippon cattle shed became The Shippon restaurant – still with its original, historic features.

Once it was up and running, the restaurant

proved very popular with caravanners and local people alike. The herringbone parlour, which we had previously planned, became a visitors' centre. It has proved a very good idea and is used by many visitors and the caravan park customers.

The interior of the shippon in February 1987 until its conversion. Below: The official opening of the Shippon Restaurant with the Mayor of Wrexham later that year.

As the restaurant was only serving meals from midday, by the following year, we felt that there was a need for a coffee shop serving coffee, light lunches and teas. And we opened up an area, which was originally a kitchen garden for The Plassey, and made it into a Tea Garden so that customers could also sit outside. This grassed area has some lovely views over the Dee Valley and is a great meeting place for visitors.

What became The Stables Coffee Shop in 1987 was the original carthorse stable where we kept both a cart horse and several pigs! The old horse stables were also converted into a storeroom for the coffee shop. The architect, Tony Minshull, told us that his wife and sister would be interested in running the new shop for us so they started it off. It became very successful and still is.

We also wanted to convert the rooms above the old stables into accommodation, but there was a

Renovating the old stables for conversion into a coffee shop.

problem: there were two huge galvanised 500-gallon tanks used for storing water up there, which we had no use for and at first, didn't know how to get down. We decided to take them out through the double doors and lower them onto a stack of bales and get them out that way. That became the Granary Flat – where the manager and his family now live.

The huge 500-gallon water tanks are carefully removed from the granary store and lifted down onto bales of hay.

Tony lends a hand with the conversion of the old grain store into a two-bedroom flat.

Meanwhile, the children were growing up and our eldest daughter, Julie, had become a jeweller, having taken a jewellery course at Wrexham Art College studying silver-smithing after completing her A-levels at Yale Sixth Form College. She went to work at a small craft centre in Farndon, Cheshire, making and designing jewellery.

After a couple of years there, she suggested carrying on her jewellery business at The Plassey. We thought that was a good idea, so we converted some of the redundant old 'calving boxes' at the front of the main farm building into craft shops, one of which she could move into, allowing her to run her business here at The Plassey, and again applied successfully for planning permission. We set Julie up in her own little workshop and it's still a jeweller's to this day. It's now run by Kerry Anne Dodd who has

Julie at her desk in her workshop at The Plassey.

occupied another workshop and has been here for over 20 years.

Julie hard at work creating her own bespoke jewellery in her workshop.

As for Jane, she decided she wanted to see more of the world before seeking to pursue a career. She went to Sweden for 12 months to work as an au pair

looking after two young children, coming home part way through to attend her graduation ceremony at Crewe and Alsager College where she received a BA degree in Combined Crafts. After this she took a

Jane in her graduation robes after receiving her degree at Crewe.

A family photograph to mark Jane's graduation. From left: John, Tony, Jane, Della and Julie.

further two jobs as au pair near London. But her love of Art remained and she was very pleased to be offered a job as a designer at Dunoon Pottery works in Stone, Staffordshire, designing coffee mugs. This was a job which she thoroughly enjoyed and she spent the next 25 years working for the company.

And John, the youngest of the three, followed in his siblings' footsteps going to the primary school at Marchwiel, but at 11, went to Ellesmere College for the next five years before going to Yale College in Wrexham to do his A-levels.

Meanwhile, work was continuing to redevelop redundant farm buildings at The Plassey. The following year saw the conversion of the old silage shed into six extra craft units, in addition to the tack room and coach house which was now a two-bedroomed self-contained cottage. We carried on converting many more of the redundant barns and now have around 15 units which are leased out to various tenants on a yearly basis.

The old coach house was converted into a cottage.

Above the restaurant kitchen were some redundant lofts originally used for grain storage and also some rooms which previously had been sleeping areas for grooms. These were the lofts that I had used for rearing chickens. We converted the lofts into a beauty studio and asked a local hairdresser called Julian Whitley if he was interested in starting his own business there. This resulted in him renting it with his wife Claire and running a very successful business for many years.

Jane and father Tony in wellington boots, ready for action.

We converted two of the Dutch barns into bad-minton courts with ping-pong tables, amusement games and a snooker table alongside. These were provided free for use by the caravanners. In 1988, an old barn (pictured opposite) was converted into what became a workshop for a picture framer.

Della on a ladder painting the sign for The Plassey Brewery. She and Tony would do much of The Plassey's routine maintenance themselves – a family tradition which has been continued.

The old barn as it looked in 1988 (top) and below, after being converted in 1989. It became the home of Eyton Framers and has been run by Phil 'the framer' for over thirty years.

A very popular feature of the caravan park started life in 1992 – The Plassey Golf Club. Tony had previously built a small pitch-and-putt course for the caravanners which was enjoyed by many and free to use. Then one day, a local businessman called Ron Brassey arrived and asked if he could design a nine-hole golf course here. Tony agreed and went into partnership for a few years.

Eventually Tony took over the running and invested quite a lot of money improving the course. The original clubhouse had the use of one small building but later another building was added with a kitchen and toilets. Each year, improvements have been made.

The Plassey's Haybank clubhouse taking shape, spring 1992.

My daughter-in-law, Sarah, now runs the Golf Club. Many social evenings are arranged by the members and they even have 'Night Golf', which is played in the dark with luminous balls!

There are also a group of seniors – comprising

older members who meet three mornings a week and special fundraising events are held with proceeds going to local charities.

In 2022 we celebrated 30 years since the Golf Club was formed. It has now grown to 125 members.

A view over the greens of the Plassey Golf Club.

CHAPTER TEN

JOHN PREPARES TO TAKE THE HELM

OUR SON John started a three-year course in Business Studies at Swansea University in 1990, graduating with a BSc (Hons) Degree in 1993. At first, after finishing it, he didn't particularly want to come home – he had hopes of getting work in the City but fellow students hadn't managed to get jobs and instead, after a lot of thought, changed his mind and he asked if he could return and help run the business.

We as parents were very happy with his decision and over the years he has gone on to be very successful as Director of The Plassey, employing around 45 people.

John with his degree certificate from Swansea: a 2:1 in Business Studies.

It was at this point in the mid-1990s that Tony and I thought it might be a good idea to build a retirement home which we could move into one day.

There was an area alongside the main farm building where former pigsties had been located which we felt would make an ideal spot for a bungalow, with lovely views over the Dee Valley. After two attempts, we obtained permission to build a dormer bungalow which we called The Whey House – named, of course, after the whey from The Plassey's cheese dairies, which had been used to feed the pigs.

The old pigsties before the Whey House was built.

John lived there after he came back from university until he decided to get married, after which he moved into the main house and we moved into the Whey House. Tony and I were quite happy to do so because it was smaller and being a dormer bungalow, more convenient.

We still have beautiful views although from a different angle. We now look more over Shropshire while the main house faces more to the West, looking into Wales.

We decided to make the grounds of the Whey House low maintenance. We didn't want a lot of up-keep in the garden so we paved a lot of it and got the groundsman from the golf course to cut the lawn areas, which were originally part of the fields. We have been very happy here.

Our eldest daughter, Julie Mary, got engaged to Robert Broad in 1998 and they married the same year. They asked us if it would be possible to use the restaurant here at The Plassey to have a civil wedding ceremony which meant obtaining a licence from the local council.

We felt the restaurant was not really suitable but there were two large rooms directly above, alongside the ones converted into a beauty salon. These had originally been used to store hay, which would make a better venue. We applied for planning permission to convert these lofts and then for a civil wedding licence. And then began the job of cleaning the lofts! This was quite a big task as they had accumulated lots of rubbish over the years which had to be cleared.

The licence came through only about a month before the wedding which was quite a relief! We had about 250 guests and a reception in a large marquee on The Plassey lawn in front of the house.

Rob and Julie on their wedding day.

Julie and Rob went to live at Emral Hall Cottage near Bangor-on-Dee, where they still are. Rob runs a mixed farm there and also breeds horses. And a few years after they moved there, they developed a small caravan touring park of their own in addition.

They had a son, Benjamin, in 2000. He celebrated his 21st in 2021 and recently graduated from Manchester Metropolitan University.

Rob and Julie help their son Ben, now aged 23, cut his cake at a party to celebrate his Christening.

John married his bride Sarah Holman at the same church as Tony and I got married in – St Mary's in Acton, Nantwich, in 2002. They had the reception in a marquee at her parents' home at Poole, near Nantwich, for about 200 guests on a lovely sunny day. Jane and her three nieces were bridesmaids.

The sun shone for the wedding of John Brookshaw and Sarah Holman. From left: Jane, John, Della, Tony, Sarah, Julie.

Their son, William Anthony, was born in 2004 followed by Zara Grace two years later in 2006. They both went to Ellesmere College. Zara is weekly boarding and did her GCSEs in 2022 before going on to do A-levels there, as William did.

Zara's Christening: John with William and Sarah with Zara.

In 2004 we embarked on another construction project at The Plassey – which proved to be a lot of fun and which Tony was particularly proud of.

We got a local builder who was very good and we suggested maybe a little lookout place. The steps which would lead up to it were already there. He said he could build something into a bit of a folly – so we went to the local builders' yards in Wrexham and found some second-hand bricks which would be good to match with the old wall because it used to be a kitchen garden originally.

The builder at first said he didn't particularly like the bricks – I think he just didn't like old, reclaimed bricks – but in the end he accepted they were perfect for the job. We just kept building the folly and adding little things like the doorway. We didn't have any plans at all, but we got to a certain height and decided that was high enough. We put in two small lookouts – viewing areas over The Plassey land and to the horizon.

We decided it would have a conical roof as we had already got one on the main house. The builder said he could do it with the help of a slater, so we got a very good slater and Tony helped too. Roland, our local plumber, put the weathervane on top using a copper ball which we found, which he said was perfect for the job.

The folly takes shape in late 2004.

The folly has been very successful. People love it. There are some of Jane's pictures of animals inside and our friend Cliff Sissons helped us put the Latin inscription of when we built it around the walls. We can see it from the Whey House and Tony used to say, 'I love that folly, that was a good idea'.

Tony hard at work creating a path to his much-loved folly.

Another of Tony's projects was the construction of a treehouse for the grandchildren in 2012. One day, he suddenly said, 'I'm going to build a treehouse.' So he used four old telegraph poles, set them in concrete, and then attached them to the trees. It was just amazing. He used spare timber from the reception on the caravan park, which we were having altered.

Tony didn't like to think it would just be cut up or burnt, he thought he might as well reuse it so that's what he did. He built the whole thing himself and we wrote Ben's name in the wet concrete. Then he said, 'I don't know how we're going to get up there.' I suggested we made the stairs at an angle, not straight up, so we did. John said once, 'I couldn't have built that treehouse like Dad did!' The grandchildren used to love playing in it when they were younger.

The treehouse built by Tony with Della's help, in 2012.

John took over the running of the caravan park and started to develop and update it, carrying on from where we had left off. We were still involved and Sarah was very capable also – we all worked together. John decided he wanted more caravans, and to create luxury pitches with electric hook-ups, so he applied for permission to use another field for this.

John didn't particularly like the farming side; he was more into the business side, while Tony was more practical, which seemed to work well. The park had got to the stage where it needed a lot of upgrading and expertise. We decided to let most of the land to local farmers and improve the golf course and other facilities.

I continued to help run the business and remained one of the directors. To the present day, I look after the plants around the craft centre and restaurant, and do a bit of weedkilling, and some of the gardening at the Whey House. I quite enjoy painting – buildings

The Plassey retail units in 2002, bedecked with flowers to mark the late Queen's Golden Jubilee. The run-down buildings have been converted into smart and thriving retail units.

not pictures! I have always been in the background if John and Sarah wanted any help with painting and cleaning, or helping with the children, babysitting, or with school runs.

I am still a partner in the business with John and Sarah. I let them run everything but I am there if they want any advice. John and Sarah have put their own personal touch to The Plassey and developed it and upgraded it so it works well. John is always keen on winning awards and getting to the top but we were the same.

We were very pleased John took over. It allowed us to take a back seat and have holidays and go and enjoy ourselves. Having said that, we enjoy it at home and we never have been too keen on travelling because we have such a lovely home and environment here. As a family we like pleasing people, letting people enjoy our surroundings and what we have created – we're happy if they're happy.

We couldn't believe that this could ever happen – from the original 'pile of bricks' – but it just materialised along the way, it wasn't something we ever dreamt would come about.

We've always been very happy with the way John and Sarah run it. John likes to make a first-class job of everything he does. We would cut corners and do things the cheaper way but he likes to be top of the tree and create a five-star park which he has done very well.

He's won lots of awards, in 2020 he won an AA award for the top park in the UK. Unfortunately it was the year when we couldn't take advantage of it because of the Pandemic.

We don't know whether William and Zara will want to carry on in the business – it's entirely up to them. I think John feels the same. If they want it, it's there. We can't predict the future and we don't particularly worry about it either.

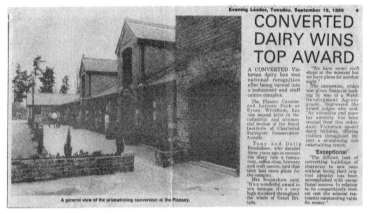

Evening Leader, Tuesday, September 19, 1989   9

CONVERTED DAIRY WINS TOP AWARD

A CONVERTED Victorian dairy has won national recognition after being turned into a restaurant and craft centre complex.

The Plassey Caravan and Leisure Park at Eyton, Wrexham, has won second prize in the industrial and commercial section of the Royal Institute of Chartered Surveyors' Conservation Awards.

Tony and Della Brookshaw, who decided three years ago to convert the dairy into a restaurant, coffee shop, brewery and craft centre, said that they had more plans for the complex.

Mrs Brookshaw said: "It's a wonderful award to win because it's a very high standard throughout the whole of Great Britain.

"We have seven craft shops at the moment but we have plans for another eight."

The conversion, which was given financial backing by way of a Welsh Development Agency grant, impressed the award judges who said: "An attractive and popular amenity has been created from this redundant Victorian model dairy building, offering visitors throughout the year a stimulating and entertaining centre.

'Exceptional'

"The difficult task of converting buildings of character to new ones without losing their original identity has been accomplished with exceptional success. In relation to its comparatively modest cost the scheme represents outstanding value for money."

A general view of the prizewinning conversion at the Plassey.

Tony and Della's achievement at converting the old dairy at The Plassey into the thriving retail centre and caravan park we know today won them numerous awards and press attention. In 1989, the Wrexham Evening Leader reported on their winning second prize in national conservation awards from the Royal Institute of Chartered Surveyors.

CHAPTER ELEVEN

MEMORABLE MOMENTS

LOOKING back, one of the great highlights of the year has always been the big annual bonfire display for Guy Fawkes Night. It all began many years ago when Tony decided to light a bonfire as a treat for the caravanners. The children all enjoyed helping to build it.

We used to hold competitions for the best guy and choose one to go on top of the bonfire. That was always an exciting time.

I can remember the first fireworks we had – we set them off in a field behind the lake. The caravanners all stood on the other side and the fireworks reflected in the water which was quite pretty. But since then we have moved it due to health and safety. It all has to be regulated and well out of reach of the visitors.

The bonfire nights are always free as it's mainly for the caravan park but we share it with local people as well, who can come along and enjoy it. It's quite an evening out for a lot of people. Some living nearby say they have a little party themselves and watch it from their own home!

Our son John insists on letting all the fireworks off. It worries me to death but he loves doing it and won't allow anyone else because you have to have certificates to be allowed to do so. He organises the display himself – he's very meticulous about it all and has staff to help in the background. We always hope for a nice, calm night with no wind.

One time, about ten years ago, John built the bonfire using tree branches and any rubbish he could find. It turned out to be a very windy night and the wind blew in the direction of the caravan park.

Lots of burning leaves from the branches floated over to the caravans and some settled on the awnings. The following morning, the caravanners found all these holes in the canvas. I don't think they were too happy!

After that, John decided only to build the bonfire with old pallets and not have anything that could fly. It was a learning curve.

One year, possibly 1987, a severe storm brought several trees down, crashing across the main drive. On this occasion, John narrowly avoided being hit by a falling beech tree.

There were quite a few funny incidents over the years. At night I used to go and check the toilets and empty the shower meters – usually at about 11 o'clock when caravanners were coming out of the Treetops bar. I remember on one occasion, I was cleaning the basins with my back towards the door and these two ladies came in.

One said to me, 'you're working late.' I said, 'oh yes,' and carried on. They went into the toilet cubicles – I think they'd had a few to drink. Then the other one whispered: 'Oh, that's the owner.'

When they came out, her friend said to me, 'I hope you get paid well, Iona.' The other lady said, 'it's not Iona it's *the owner!*' She replied in astonishment, 'are you the owner?' I said 'yes', and she exclaimed in horror, 'and you're cleaning the toilets?' I nodded

Della and Tony always enjoyed getting involved in activities they would put on for caravanners. Here, they are organising a sweepstake.

and they both went out laughing.

Tony and I have always been hands-on. A while ago, I was brushing up and this chap said, 'excuse me, love, how long have you been working here?' I said, '60 years'. He said, 'brushing up for 60 years?' I said, 'oh yes,' and he just carried on. I think he felt quite sorry for me. We've had lots of laughs like that.

One night the electricity went off and of course it left all the toilets in darkness. I decided to put candles in the toilets and a lady came up to me next morning and said, 'those candles were dangerous, that's health and safety.' I said we had no choice but to do it. She replied, 'well, it cost us – you took money off us for the electric for the night and we didn't have electric'. I pointed out that it wasn't our fault and we couldn't help it. She insisted on having her money back and pointing out how dangerous those candles were.

In the end I said 'look, the best thing is to go to a solicitor,' and she said, 'I *am* a solicitor.' Whether that was true I don't know but we've not heard from her since! You have to laugh off these things and carry on. In the main, the caravanners have been wonderful and we've always treated them as one of us. We have always joined in all the activities which we would organise for August Bank Holiday Weekend when the park would be full.

A popular event was our Miss Plassey competition. Every year, around 20 girls would do their hair and line up. I would make a Miss Plassey sash with the year on it and we would get people to judge them

and choose the winner and runners-up. I think my
mother one year was the judge. One of the caravanners had a florist's business so she would make three
little bouquets for first, second and third prize and

On August Bank Holiday weekend, such as this one in 1988,
Della and Tony would organise a range of fun activities and
prize-winning competitions for the caravanners.

we would give them out with little prizes and a cup. The contestants would think the world of this cup. This went on for a number of years. Parents would go to so much trouble to get their daughters dolled up and there was always quite a lot of jealousy and rivalry, of course!

In another event, the men dressed up as ladies in dresses and funny bras and pants and we had ladies versus gents football matches which ended up in a water fight with the players getting buckets of water and throwing them over each other.

And then we had tossing the caber – Tony found a tree trunk and made it into a caber which was fun. Another highlight we called walking on water – we would go down to the lake and tie a row of pallets together and the contestants would have to run across the water on the pallets with an opponent trying to stop them, until of course they fell in!

We had competitions for the children like wheelbarrow races, egg and spoon races and throwing an egg. You put them in rows and they would start close together throwing a real egg between each other and then get further and further away. On one occasion we realised that the winner had actually got a hard-boiled egg!

Caravanners would come back year after year – some would come every weekend. I remember in particular these six people from Runcorn and Wallasey – every Friday night straight after work they would arrive at The Plassey and help with anything we wanted and Sunday night they would go home.

It was wonderful, they loved it.

It became a really nice community. A lady called Mary used to help me run the shop on the caravan park and when I took on the coffee shop she would come and help me with that. They never wanted money, they just loved it and in exchange, we used to give them free caravanning – it was their second home. The caravanners built a treehouse for the children and we had lots of fun having raft races on the Dee on specially-built rafts.

There was always something going on. Even now those same people will often come back – sometimes with their grandchildren and recall taking part and saying they were Miss Plassey or something. They would call The Plassey their second home and probably many still do.

It's been our life for 60 years and we love it, we love meeting people from different backgrounds. Someone came up to Tony a while ago and said, 'we have been coming here 50 years!' And now their children and grandchildren come.

CHAPTER TWELVE

HOLIDAYS

OVER the years, we had many lovely holidays with our children throughout their childhood. One of our first was taking the girls to stay in a touring caravan in Aberdaron when they were three and five years of age. I think this helped to give us the idea of having caravans at our farm in the future!

We had a memorable holiday to Spain in the early 1970s with our friends Janet and Bernard Owens. It was our first-ever wine-tasting tour, to the Burgundy region. We were travelling around, visiting the vineyards.

We stopped where they were picking grapes and they would chat to us about how they picked them and which winery they took them to, to crush the grapes.

They handed me a bottle to try and I couldn't see any glasses so I just drank from the bottle and they thought it was quite funny! I think it was a good wine. I can't remember what variety it was but I know it was a red, as they were picking black grapes! (*See overleaf.*)

Our first trip abroad with the three children was to a hotel in Torremolinos in Spain. We also visited

Madeira and then decided to purchase a chalet at Abersoch on the North Wales coast.

Della enjoys a swig of the local red wine as her friend Janet Owens (on the far left) looks on in amusement!

Della amid the vines on the wine-tasting tour in Burgundy with Tony and friends Janet and Bernard Owens.

At Abersoch, late 1960s. From left: Jane, Julie, Tony, Tim Brookshaw, Granny Mabel Brookshaw, Della's mother May Cooke, Grandpa Stanley Brookshaw, Susan Cooke (now Okell, Della's niece; Jill Brookshaw, Tony's niece.

Also at Abersoch with friends. From left: Claire, Janet, Julie Brookshaw, Eldon, Jane Brookshaw, Karen, Tony and Della, Alison Jenkins, John Brookshaw (at the front).

After a few years the children were getting bored with going to Abersoch, so we sold the chalet and went further afield. We decided to try skiing.

That first skiing holiday came about after talking to some friends who had been and we thought it sounded fun. I was in Wrexham one day and decided to go into the travel agents and ask about skiing.

The owner suggested we go to Davos in Switzerland if we hadn't skied before. I said that I didn't know whether we would take to it or not. He recommended checking into a five-star hotel which we could enjoy, if we didn't like the skiing itself.

We took his advice and booked a week in Davos. Julie didn't come it was just the four of us, Tony and I, Jane and John.

We got our ski equipment – salopettes and big, insulated ski boots – moon boots they called them in those days. We decided we might as well go in our outfits but when we got to the airport, nobody else

A slightly-blurred photo of Tony, John and Della in Davos, on their first-ever family skiing holiday.

had got ski outfits on, yet they must have been going skiing. We realised that people don't don their ski gear to go on the plane! And we were so hot on the flight with our big snow boots on.

We laughed when we got to the hotel because we were all dolled up and somebody said, 'oh are you going skiing!' On a train to the actual resort, up in the mountains, I heard these people talking about their 'bindings' and I thought 'whatever are bindings?' I didn't want to ask. Anyway we learnt a lot when we got skiing. We found out that they were to hold the ski boots on to the skis.

Our hotel was very smart but John wasn't keen on the food. He was very particular about food, so he would never come down to dinner at night, all he would have was chips and a sort of cream custard for pudding. That was all he had each night! He would have been about nine at the time. It was difficult for John because we all had to have skiing instruction – John went into the junior ski school and he had a German-speaking ski instructor. All the other children could speak fluent German and of course, he couldn't!

While in Davos we chatted to a couple at the next

Della and Tony, also taken on their first-ever skiing holiday to Davos.

table – they said that they came every year – she skied but her husband wouldn't do so. He had his own business as a dental surgeon and was always frightened of breaking something because being self-employed he couldn't afford to do so. But one night we noticed at dinner his arm was in a sling and we asked what had happened.

He replied, 'oh, I slipped on the ice outside, on the pavement.' His wife said that she couldn't help but laugh as he was the one who refused to ski!

The following year we decided to go somewhere more casual. We had learnt that you don't go in your ski outfits and you don't go to smart hotels but to hotels where they do a lot of après-ski and are more relaxed.

That first time we had been complete novices; we had no idea what to expect and all our farming friends thought it was stupid going skiing because it was so cold and horrible, and yet now we hear that our friends' children all go, it is so different these days.

One year, we decided to go skiing to Austria to celebrate Christmas and New Year over there, since we had heard their festive celebrations were always very good.

We stayed in a lovely hotel and I always remember them lighting real candles on the Christmas tree which we never had because they were too dangerous but it was lovely watching them. In total we had about six skiing holidays and thoroughly enjoyed them.

Skiing holidays over the years: Top left: Della and Tony. Top right: Julie and Della. Left, on the toboggan run: Julie, Della and Tony. Bottom: in Seefeld, Austria. From left: family friends Anne and Joe Hamlett, Julie, family friend Iona, and Tony.

In 1979 we met a lovely lady called Mary Lufkin from Minneapolis-Saint Paul who was a member of an American choir. We got to know her through the hospitality committee for the International Eisteddfod in Llangollen – she was performing at the Eisteddfod and came to lodge with us at The Plassey.

We got on very well and she invited us all to stay at her home in Minneapolis over Christmas. We normally only take one week's holiday a year but managed ten days visiting America! It was a wonderful experience meeting lots of her many friends and family.

Jane, John, Della and Tony on their Christmas holiday in America as guests of the Lufkin family.

One evening we had a great storm and a large snowfall, and we woke to about 15 inches of snow! This was unusual at Christmas. Mary has been back since to stay with us here in Wales and in fact, recently came to stay with me (April 2022).

A sleigh ride while on holiday in America with the Lufkins.

One holiday which stands out was our ten-day cruise on the QE2 in 2006. We flew from Manchester to Southampton and then took the QE2 along the coast and then up to Norway. The actual ship itself was getting a bit tired, it was quite shabby and the lifts were slow. I think they decommissioned it two years later.

But the food was wonderful – we went with friends, Cindy McAlpine and Chris Bell, who had a deluxe cabin with a balcony. There were three dining rooms depending on what class you were in. We were in the second class and they were in first. They asked the staff if we could go into their dining room.

They said no, but our friends could come to our dining room and they would put us on the Captain's table each evening which was rather nice. We always had a member of the crew on the table and free wine all evening, so we thoroughly enjoyed that.

Tony and I went to Nice in France, again with Cindy and Chris, and this was followed with coach holidays to Spain, Italy, and Greece with our friends Dianne and Dr Cliff Sissons.

A holiday to remember: Tony and Della Brookshaw on their
ten-day cruise to Norway on the QE2 in 2006.

Our most recent holiday with Cliff and Di was a few days in Jersey a couple of years ago. Portmeirion is another of our favourite holiday destinations.

My cousins Bernard and Margaret Byrd joined us there in 2009 for a couple of nights. We enjoyed their company and have had a couple of visits to London, staying at the Farmers Club. We also went with them to Northern Ireland in 2017 together with our life-long friends, Bill and Thelma Windsor.

Tony with Cliff and Di on holiday in Greece.

Tony, Cliff and Di Sissons on holiday in
spring 2008, in possibly Spain or Greece.

Top: Della and life-long friend Jill Johnson, formerly Cooper, on holiday at The Warren, Abersoch. Left: Tony and Della at Powis Castle, and below, on a winter skiing holiday.

Della and Tony enjoying lunch on holiday in Nice, with their friends Chris Bell and Cindy McAlpine.

Above left: At the Giant's Causeway, Northern Ireland, in 2017. From left: Margaret Byrd, Bernard Byrd, Thelma Windsor, Della, Bill Windsor, Tony.
Above right: Tony and Della on holiday in Venice.

Della and Tony on holiday in Greece.

Anne Hamlett and Jane on a surprise day trip to Venice that Anne put on as a treat for Della and Jane.

Della and Tony on holiday in Holland with friends Bert and Tina de Jongh, having a coffee in Amsterdam.

CHAPTER THIRTEEN

PARTIES AND CELEBRATIONS

W E HAVE always loved entertaining and sharing with friends – laying on lots of dinner parties and celebrations for important birthday parties and special wedding anniversaries, all the milestones!

Tony and I gave many parties around the lovely table in our dining room. The dining room in my house at The Plassey was a hallowed place. Its door was almost always shut and we ate in it as a family only on special occasions and sometimes for Sunday lunch. When we had a dinner party, the children would all wait at the top of the stairs for us to retire to the lounge and then sneak downstairs to eat what was left – especially the puddings!

Lunch at Plas Talgarth, Machynlleth. From left: Ann Hamlett, David Jenkins, Joe Hamlett, Della, Carol Jenkins, Tony.

Dinner party in the main house at The Plassey – probably 1979. From left: Eifion Ellis, Neville Rees (his brother Ken was in The Great Escape), Mary Lufkin, Tony, Della, Eira Ellis, Professor Stephenson, Thelma Rees.

Tony, Jane, Della and John with Mary Lufkin and her late husband Jim, on their first visit to Wales in July 1979, when they stayed at The Plassey for the Eisteddfod at Llangollen.

One Christmas we managed to seat 20 people. I remember I made one large Christmas pudding and a guest remarked it was the biggest pudding she had ever seen! We entertained many overseas visitors. One year our American friend Mary Lufkin, who was staying with us, introduced us to a local choir from Rhos here in Wales and we invited about 12 of them into our house.

On another occasion with some American visitors, we arranged a dinner party for them and afterwards, Tony and I sang We're a Couple of Swells – much to their amusement!

New Year's Eve has often been celebrated with our friends and relatives here at The Plassey. One party nearly ended in disaster when our friend Bill Windsor opened the wrong door and ended up at the bottom of the cellar steps! Luckily, he had no injuries except for a small tear in his trousers.

Christmas has always been a happy family time, with all the family gathering together for Christmas Day. I enjoyed cooking the turkey dinner and the children would hand out the many presents after

Christmas lunch, from left: Auntie Ena Harris, Julie, Rob, Della, Tony, John, Andrew Enoch, and Jane.

Christmas Day lunch, probably 2000. From left: Julie, Rob, Tony, John, Della holding baby Ben.

lunch. Boxing Day is also a family day but we invite friends and neighbours along too, in the evening.

One of the adults might dress up as Father Christmas and hand out presents. We often ended up playing charades with everyone taking a turn.

Another gathering for Christmas lunch, clockwise from left: Rob, Jane, Zara, Mrs Bernice Holman (Sarah's mother), Sarah, William, Ben, Tony, Della, John, circa 2017 or 2018.

Family gathering in the 1960s: Jim Harris (Della's brother); grandmother Eva Harris; Auntie May (Gibson); Della; sister-in-law Barbara carrying baby Stephen; Father Christmas Gerald Harris (Della's mother's brother; Della's mother May.

Marking the various milestone birthdays and anniversaries has been very important to us over the years and a good excuse to throw a big party!

In 2000 for our Ruby Wedding anniversary, we had

Tony and Della celebrate their Ruby Wedding in 2000.

about 80 people with a marquee on the front lawn. We had caterers in and music. It was a nice day so we were able to stand outside and have champagne.

Ruby Wedding guests, from left: Ina Walsh, Bert de Jongh, Jenny and John Sutton, Pat Minshull, Tina de Jongh.

Jane, Julie and John paid for their parents to go for a surprise two-night trip to Paris to mark their Ruby Wedding.

Tony and Della at Versailles Palace on their anniversary break in Paris.

We had a marquee on the lawn for a party to mark the christening of our granddaughter Zara in September 2006:

In a marquee on the lawn for Zara's christening party in September 2006. Della with old school friend Jill Johnson; Tony sitting next to Jill's husband Michael Johnson.

My 70th birthday party was held at Bangor-on-Dee racecourse on a wartime theme as I was born in 1938, just before the outbreak of war.

We had about 100 guests and as they arrived, we played a recording of the old air-raid siren and gave them a spoof menu, with dishes like tripe and onions and freshly-caught rabbit, pobs and spotted dick and custard for pudding. People didn't know what pobs

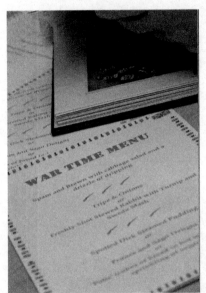

were – they are cubes of white bread and hot milk. I can remember my father eating them when I was a young child. One or two guests said, 'we don't particularly like tripe and onions!'

The spoof wartime menu offering up such delicacies as tripe and onions, "pobs" and spotted dick!

Tony takes the microphone to speak a few words at Della's 70th birthday party. He clearly said something amusing!

At first they thought it was for real but they laughed when they realised it was just a joke! We put up lots of Union Jack flags and sang plenty of war-time songs, it was a lot of fun.

A family photo to mark Della's 70th. From left: Jane, Rob Broad, William, Julie, Tony, Della, Ben, Sarah, Zara and John.

For our Golden Wedding Anniversary in 2010, we had a marquee on the lawn outside the Whey House and a catering firm to do a meal. I think there were about 80 people here – it was lovely weather and all the hydrangeas were out along the wall.

We had some bridesmaids there, those who were left. I think there were about five of us on the same table. We had a lovely meal and speeches – it was a very nice day.

Della and Tony prepare to cut the cake to mark their Golden
Wedding Anniversary in 2010 in a marquee on the lawn.

Grand-
children
William,
Zara and
Ben sitting
on the grass
at the party.

For Tony's 80th birthday in 2014, we had about 20 friends over for a luncheon. I thought a good present for him would be to get the clock chimes on the tower above the Shippon restaurant working again as a surprise.

We had originally installed the clock ourselves – Tony's mother Mabel Brookshaw left me a legacy of some money in her will and Tony was always a stickler for time so I had the idea of using the money to put a clock on the tower outside. It would strike every hour and quarter hour.

Whenever it chimed, Tony would always say, 'Mother says it's such and such a time.' But after about ten years, the actual chimes stopped, although the clock itself carried on working. We never thought about restoring it but then it occurred to me that Tony's 80th birthday would be the ideal time.

Tony in front of the restored clock on his 80th birthday.

We had a job to get it done because every time the clock repairers came to sort the workings out and have a rehearsal, Tony happened to be outside. I had to get him inside so he didn't hear it!

On his birthday, I invited guests with the plan to take him outside to listen to the chimes at 12 noon. We just managed at the last second to get him outside and he said, 'what's that?' and I said, 'that's the clock!' 'Good heavens!' he said. 'Who's done that?' He was astonished to hear it again. Now it chimes every quarter of an hour, just like it always did.

In 2018 I celebrated my 80th birthday with afternoon tea at the Grosvenor Hotel in Pulford with

Tony and Della at a party to mark Della's 80th birthday in 2018.

about 12 friends. I left Tony at home because it was only ladies but all of a sudden he arrived out of nowhere! I told him we weren't expecting him and he replied that he thought he would just join us anyway.

Then all of a sudden John walked in with a cake and balloons and said, 'I've come to wish you a happy birthday!' They had kept it completely secret from me, I had no idea. I had already taken a chocolate cake but they came with this wonderful, iced cake, especially done for my 80th birthday. They were always up to tricks! We all had a celebration drink together. It was a very nice surprise.

We celebrated our Diamond wedding anniversary during the Pandemic, so I'll come back to it in the next chapter. Marking these milestones has always been important to us and my side of the family have always been keen to have family reunions, especially at Christmas time, and we would have Father Christmas visiting on each occasion.

Every year, during my early years, we held Cousins' Parties – there were usually about 20 of us who met up at our own homes and reminisced on all our family parties going back to childhood. I remember one year, my Father dressing up as Father Christmas. Most of my relatives were farmers and we were all assembled at an uncle's farmhouse where we would look through the window to see Santa coming up the drive with a sack on his back.

He would distribute the presents and that was always something to look forward to. Ever since then we have carried on with the tradition of cousins' parties – unfortunately during the two-year Pandemic we weren't able to get together the same but that's the next party we will have to arrange.

Another longstanding tradition is holding New Year's Eve parties. The New Year's Eve crowd originally consisted of 18 friends – going back about 25 years to when we first got together. Over the years many have sadly passed on and I think we're left with nine of the 18 but we still meet up – not on the evening of New Year's Eve as we used to, but for luncheons now and usually at a restaurant or hotel, rather than entertaining at our own homes. That's what we've been doing the last ten years.

'New Year's Eve' friends get-together, from left: Roy Willis, Joyce Williams, Hazel Willis, Bernard Byrd, Margaret Byrd, Kay Cope, Janet Rowland, Geoff Cope, Bill Windsor, John Rowland, Thelma Windsor, Bernard Mulliner, Rosemary Mulliner, Bob Jones, Hazel Jones, Tony and Della.

Cousins' party: Patrick Newbrook, Vanessa Newbrook, Della, Tony, Ian Byrd, Jane, Fred West, Pat Peake, Clive Woodward, Hazel Woodward, Margaret Parton, Anne Furnival, Stella Byrd, Fred Furnival, Sidney Byrd, Eleanor Halfpenny, Pat Timmis, Neil Cooke, Margaret Byrd, John Timmis, Bernard Byrd.

Tony and Della in France as guests of Tony's cousin Patrick Newbrook and wife Vanessa, for daughter Stephanie's marriage to Gavin Clements, June 2007.

CHAPTER FOURTEEN

RECENT TIMES

OVER the years we have rarely had any disgruntled customers but a few years ago, someone with an apparent grudge against us caused thousands of pounds of damage – and was only caught thanks to John's quick thinking.

We were refurbishing the restaurant at the time. One night, we heard a lot of noise outside. It was about two o' clock in the morning. We went to look. Patio lights had been smashed at the front of the Whey House. I rang John and spoke to Sarah. I said I thought there was somebody about because some of our lights had been smashed and garden furniture strewn around the front of the house.

She went to get John and, as it happened, Tony was up doing a crossword, which he often did in the night. The two of us went over to the main house. John went up to the caravan park. He came back and said, 'you and Dad get back quick, I can see somebody walking around up there.' So he ordered us back into the house for safety.

John shot off in the pick-up to see if he could see anyone. Sarah said she could hear an awful lot of banging noises outside, but we didn't dare go and have a look at what was happening in case we were hurt. John came back and by this time there were five police cars here – but in the meantime he found this person and chased him down to the crossroads and managed to grab him – before the police got here.

The vandal did thousands of pounds' damage in a wrecking spree which included smashing the swimming pool windows and the urns outside.

John kept him on the floor until the police arrived and handcuffed him. The vandal had done a huge amount of damage – he knocked over all the flower urns and smashed windows in the swimming pool, toilets and shops.

We just couldn't believe what had happened. Subsequently, when he appeared in court, it turned out that he was a known criminal and drug addict who had been in prison a number of times. He was local, I think from Wrexham. But we had never come across him before and couldn't understand his motive. However, prior to that, we had had a burglary in the restaurant when we were renovating it and a lot of tools belonging to the workers were taken and many of the shops broken into. We wondered whether it was retaliation for all that. Because again on that occasion, John had chased the people in a van and caught up with them. Thanks to him the police were able to stop and question them but they claimed they were off to a job in Shrewsbury and the police let them go!

In all, the vandal had caused about £4,000 of damage but what was especially frightening was that when Sarah opened the front door, she found three bunches of dead flowers on the doorstep. It was all such a mystery. Fortunately, we've never seen anything of him since!

During the Pandemic, we couldn't have any people visiting. The retail park and craft centre had to close; the golf club had to close; as did the caravan park, swimming pool and restaurant – everything had to shut down. John employs about 45 full and part-time staff and a lot were put on furlough.

A few he retained to keep the place smart. We just carried on upgrading on the park and doing some painting and cleaning. Eventually we were allowed to open again but then there was another lockdown, which was devastating for our trade. Fortunately, we had one or two grants which helped.

It was very strange, having been used to people whenever you went outside, there was always somebody around to chat to. But during the Pandemic, that all stopped. We carried on, keeping ourselves busy, we still had the sheep and the cattle in the fields but no people! The important thing was to battle on and keep going.

The ornamental sheep painted by Jane in the deserted Tea Garden at The Plassey during the Pandemic – sensibly wearing a face mask!

On July 23rd, 2020, Tony and I celebrated our Diamond Wedding Anniversary. Because of the lockdown restrictions, we were only allowed 20 guests, otherwise, knowing us, we would have had quite a big party. We hired a small marquee for the garden at the Whey House and just invited our close family

Tony and Della celebrating their Diamond Wedding
Anniversary in July 2020, under Covid restrictions.

and friends. It was a shame because we would have loved a big party to celebrate 60 years of marriage and living at The Plassey.

It wasn't to be but at least we *did* celebrate and enjoyed it and the weather was good. That was our last party really. Also we received a lovely card from the late Queen to

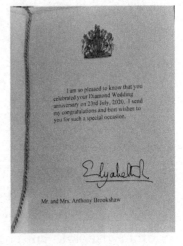

mark the occasion, which John helped organise. He had to send our marriage certificate as proof!

Della in the marquee for her special wedding anniversary with longstanding family friend, Lieutenant Colonel Jamie Balls. Below, Tony and Della (on the right) with guests from left, Michael and Jill Johnson, Nick Jenkins and his mother Carol Jenkins.

In 2021, the Shippon restaurant reopened under new management as the BLK Sheep Bar and Grill – we knew it as the Black Sheep but because of copyright they couldn't actually call it that.

It proved a great success but sadly, it wasn't to last. The Pandemic made it a struggle for them to recruit staff and in the end they gave up the lease. I'll come back to the latest on the restaurant in the final chapter.

CHAPTER FIFTEEN

SAD DEATH OF TONY

IT WAS during the later stages of writing this autobiography that we suffered a huge blow: the unexpected death of my husband, Tony. He died on January 7th 2022 at the age of 87 after a short illness. It all seemed to happen very quickly.

We celebrated Christmas 2021 as a family here at the Whey House – there were ten of us sitting around the table. Tony did seem quiet on Christmas Day, and had become a bit weaker with his walking, but we didn't think anything of it, really.

It was on 29th December that he complained that his chest was feeling a bit tight and he was having a lot of difficulty breathing. John came over and rang 999. They sent paramedics who said his oxygen levels were very low and they suspected he had pneumonia.

They gave him oxygen for about an hour. Then another paramedic came and said he should go to hospital. John rang our friend Dr Cliff Sissons, a cardiologist. Cliff thought he should go for an X-ray to see what the problem was.

Tony was taken to the Maelor Hospital in Wrexham for X-rays and scans and at that time I wasn't allowed to go and see him because of Covid. He was taken first to A&E and then to ICU, then the next time we got through they said he was on Fleming Ward but we couldn't see him 'until we say so'.

In the end, a friend and neighbour of Jane's managed to get in touch with somebody senior at the hospital who said we could see him in the corridor. So Jane and I went to the hospital and eventually were able to chat to him. He had to come off the oxygen to be able to speak to us and I could see he needed it, so we didn't keep him too long.

Soon after, we had a phone call from the hospital asking us to go in which I thought sounded pretty serious. We rushed off there in a panic, but when we got there the nurses refused to let us into the ward until we had filled in a questionnaire and undergone a Covid test. It was quite traumatic because we were so anxious to see him.

We then had to wait half an hour for the result of the test and all this time I was thinking, is he still alive? Finally, we got to see him and John and I were there most of the night with him. There was so much noise in the ward, but eventually they moved him to a side room which was more private. Jane, John and Julie came back regularly to visit him and I never left his side.

I had decided I was going to stay there day and night. Jane and John's wife Sarah brought me in some extra clothes and food. I was very well looked after, the children were so kind. Eventually, on Tony's last night, John said 'look mum, you have got to have some sort of bed to lie on, you can't just sit in that chair all day and night'. So they arranged to get a bed, from the children's ward, I think, so I had somewhere to sleep.

John said, 'that must be heaven for you tonight, to have a bed.' Then all of a sudden we looked at Tony and his breathing was going slower, and I said that I thought he was going. And he was.

John believes it was because his father knew I was settled and comfortable and he was ready to go, so he just quietly went. That was about quarter past eleven on the seventh of January, 2022. So in the end, it was all so peaceful.

One of the last things he said to me was, 'enjoy yourself, Dell, and when I'm gone, make sure you have a damn good piss-up!'

The funeral went well and fortunately it was just as the Covid restrictions on large gatherings were coming to an end. There were 200 at the church and 100 at least at the wake and we had a very good, happy send-off – which is what he would have wanted. He always said, at any funeral we went to, 'I hope mine's a bit better than this!'

We were spaced out in the church and the vicar was very fussy about people keeping their distance but of course when we got back to The Plassey and gathered in the restaurant, everybody was kissing and hugging. It was such a poignant moment when we arrived back from church because the chimes of his clock were striking and despite everything, there was all this happiness but I am quite sure he would have approved!

Tony was adamant that if anything happened to him, I was to go off and enjoy myself so I booked a holiday with Jane – a cruise down the coast of Spain for 12 days. It was very sad without him as we had been together all the time. But it's important to remember all that we shared together. We had lots of lovely holidays and parties.

As you'll appreciate from this book, Tony and I had a wonderful life – great happiness and a wonderful family and that's what we have got to be thankful for.

A recent photograph of Tony's much-loved Folly under a thick layer of snow with the daffodils that Della planted coming up in front of it, representing the circle of life.

CHAPTER SIXTEEN

LIFE GOES ON

WORK continues to develop and update The Plassey. John is converting the old dairies attached to the main house where they used to make the cheese and where some of the staff used to stay when it was still a farm.

Tony and I had originally converted them into what we called the Top Flat, Bottom Flat and Tower Flat, which used to be the billiard room. But John is knocking through the wall to incorporate the Tower Flat into the Top Flat, to make one larger flat. He is making the rooms more modern – they were always very gloomy and draughty because they face north, which was ideal for cheese-making but not for living accommodation.

Because they were dairies originally, John has come across one or two problems. The workmen discovered a big, eight-foot deep tank under the living room of the Bottom Flat, intended for storing rain water to use in the house. They are now having to fill it in with rubble because of the risk of damp.

It was in the basement beneath the living room and was originally where they used to have the boiler to heat the water to scald all the vessels for making the cheese.

The Bottom Flat will incorporate one of our old pantries which was used originally to salt the pork in a trough after killing the pig. That is now going to be part of the heating system for the two flats.

John has gone up-to-date with ground-source heating for the flats. They have put pipes in about a metre down which uses the heat from the ground to heat the water. It's expensive to install but in the future will mean free hot water.

We are lucky to have the land on the front field to incorporate all this – without land we wouldn't be able to do it. My old pantry, the one that featured in the magazine, is still there, but it hasn't got any old pickles in it now!

In the future, we're hoping that the manager of The Plassey and his family will live in the Top Flat and Sarah is hoping that her mother, who still lives in Nantwich, will retire to the Bottom Flat, which will be more convenient for her.

A digger at work on The Plassey field in October 2023, installing pipes to provide free heat from the ground.

At the moment, we have scaffolding up on the main house. John decided to put in new windows and replace the old pebbledash. He plans to put a new roof on with new slates – it probably hasn't been done since the 1900s and slates don't last forever.

The roof and walls will be much better insulated and should retain the heat a lot better.

The brick-built tower on the main house was originally a water tower – for storing water for use in the main house. This water was pumped up from a

Scaffolding on the main house at The Plassey, in October 2023.

windmill which is situated in the front field. The tank is slate-lined and although it is no longer used it is still in the tower. We now have a mains water supply of course.

I let him get on with it – Tony and I always did what we wanted and Mother-in-law used to come and look and would always say: 'it's all right if you can afford it.' We were ahead of our time developing the farm buildings and introducing the leisure side of it with the caravans and John has inherited our enthusiasm for modernising buildings and preserving them and bringing them up to date, as we would do.

The restaurant has been closed now for about 18 months. The people who came in to run it were having a lot of problems and the manager announced that he wanted to go elsewhere and they decided to give it up. The aftermath of Covid didn't help.

We are painting it and cleaning it and hope to advertise it shortly and get people in to lease it later in 2024, ready for the holiday season. The caravanners enjoyed the restaurant and miss it and it was a good chance through the winter to get it set up again. In the meantime, they have still got the golf club for more informal meals and the little coffee shop, which is always popular.

We are still feeling the effects of the Pandemic at The Plassey, especially with the restaurant currently closed. People enjoyed coming up for lunch and looking round the shops at the same time but since Covid, they don't seem to go out as much as they used to. There's the cost of living crisis at the moment and many people are now working from home and ordering shopping online.

Also the nature of the businesses here has changed – we don't get as many doing crafts today, now it is mainly those offering services, like hairdressers and chiropodists.

Nonetheless, the retail units are still doing well and many shoppers enjoy coming here rather than going into town because of all the problems with parking and traffic. It's easy and free to park here and I think that encourages people to come here and they like to have a bite to eat in the coffee shop or the golf clubhouse, or wander around and have a

Decades of hard work at The Plassey continue to be recognised with industry awards. Della, son John and wife Sarah are pictured with the Peniarth Estate Silver Trowel for winning the Farm Buildings and Works Competition at the Royal Welsh Show in July 2022.

stroll – we've got a nice walk which is open to the public around the fields, and the play area is also open to the public. They can bring the children here and have an ice cream from the ice cream shop. So all in all it's a nice day out for everybody. The golf course also brings a lot of people up here.

The Plassey retail park, basking in summer sunshine, bedecked with flowers and hanging baskets.

The retail units are open 12 months a year, with the caravan park just closed for a short period during December and January. So although we're not as busy as we have been in the past, we're very fortunate compared to most other shopping centres and the caravan park remains very popular.

John's wife Sarah runs the Golf Club – she's the Lady Captain and really enjoys playing and their

John and Sarah Brookshaw with their children
William (in his prefect's gown) and Zara on the
last day of term at Ellesmere College in 2021.

daughter Zara does as well. Hopefully in the future,
John and Sarah's children William and Zara will take
The Plassey on. William is now 20 and is currently in
his second year at Cardiff University doing Business

William, as a Sixth Form prefect at Ellesmere.

Studies. Zara is 18 and in the Upper Sixth at Ellesmere, doing A-levels. She is keen on Art – she wants to go down that route, like my daughter Jane. Zara must have that in her genes! I think she is hoping to go to university eventually.

She's quite sporty and plays hockey, netball and golf, and is also in the choir at Ellesmere which she's enjoying. She's been made a prefect for this last year which has given her responsibility as well.

Zara in her prefect's gown at Ellesmere College in 2023, where she is currently doing her A-levels.

Ben with his degree in banking from Manchester Metropolitan.

Julie and Rob's son Ben got his degree in banking in 2023 at Manchester Metropolitan University. He decided to stay in Manchester, so he rented a flat with his girlfriend Kaitlin who is still in her last year doing speech therapy. They share this flat which is 36 floors up, which he loves. Coming from the countryside – it's unbelievable!

Ben with his girlfriend Kaitlin and his parents, Rob and Julie Broad, enjoying a family meal out.

After graduating, Ben got a job in Altrincham with a financial company that do loans, which he is enjoying. I think there are only about 35 employees. He goes there by car each morning. He enjoys banking and finance and the city life.

Losing Tony has left a huge gap in my life but there's always somebody to talk to and John comes in two or three times a week to have a chat. My daughters Jane and Julie go to keep fit on Tuesday and Thursday evening and they'll pop in afterwards.

I just keep myself busy, there's always something to do! Luckily I have got family close by and lots of friends, especially the Bramblewood Close community in Overton who have enrolled me in their parties which is lovely because it is nice to have friends who are always there and it's been great for Jane because

The Bramblewood club enjoying Della's excellent hospitality at The Whey House in January, 2024. Daughter Jane is taking the photograph. From left: Robert Davies, Anne Williams, Alun Gwatkin, Kate Davies, Mark Williams, Della (standing), Sally Gwatkin and David Williams.

she's not isolated, living on her own.

I have always got friends here at The Plassey and if I just want to pop out and have a chat to somebody, there's usually someone to chat to. I usually ask if they are staying here on the site.

Visitors often like to talk about The Plassey and hear about how Tony and I developed the park in the past. I have got a little community here and also I love to be able to drive still – without my little car to go around in I would be quite lost!

Recently I went to see a relation of Tony's – his sister's husband, Tony Taylor. He lived over in Calverhall, on the other side of Whitchurch and has only just died, aged 98. He lived on his own and was always pleased to see me. His last words to me as I left that final time were, 'you must find yourself a man!' I said, 'no, I've had my man for over 60 years!'

We were looking at all the old photograph albums – going over the weddings and the guests and he enjoyed that, remembering all the guests at those weddings. He didn't have much company really. I would go to see him about every two or three weeks.

I called at my daughter Julie's on the way and took a young walnut tree, about a metre high. It was one I found amongst all the shrubs – because we have a mature walnut tree here, in the tea garden, the squirrels take the nuts and plant them, then of course, some grow into trees. And they haven't got any walnut trees at Emral where Julie lives. I've pickled walnuts in the past – unfortunately John pruned the tree a couple of years ago and it's only just beginning to produce walnuts again so I haven't been able to pickle any for a while! A lot of people don't actually like them and sometimes people say, what are these black things? I think originally there was one walnut tree here in the wood, and I have planted two, John cut one down because it was in the way of the drive, so now there is only the one in the tea garden. We have got a variety of trees in the tea garden – the walnut tree, a mulberry tree, pear trees, apple trees and a fig tree. There are quite a few unusual species, and they all bear fruit. The mulberry tree especially every year – but I think the starlings finish the mulberries off. I found a bottle of mulberry wine the other day dating back to the 60s or 70s, I think it is still okay!

A get-together with former members of the now-closed Erbistock WI, to mark the late Queen's Platinum Jubilee in 2022. From left: Iola Roberts, Della Brookshaw, Lucy Haar, Gwenan Done, and Sheila Lewis.

When we came here, there was a peach tree with actual peaches on it, against a south-facing wall. I have a photograph of me picking the peaches. Sadly it has since died. We get masses of figs on our fig tree but they don't ripen, it's too cold.

Losing Tony has changed my life completely but you have to accept it for the sake of the family and get on with life, and be pleased that you are able to do so and lucky to have good health. My mother was only 45 when my father died. I have had a lot more years with my husband than she did. I'm grateful for that.

Tony would always say, if anything happened to him, to enjoy myself – it was definitely what he wanted for me – he didn't want me to mourn. He was always one to enjoy himself and wanting other people to do the same. He wasn't selfish, he was very grateful for what he had and what we did together.

That is a source of strength to me. I don't feel guilty if I go on holiday and enjoy myself because that's what Tony would have wished for me, and he also liked me to help other people and make them happy – giving parties and all the rest of it.

I still enjoy cooking and love to give parties and make Sunday lunches. If I do get bored on a very wet day, for instance, I will think, I'll go and bake a cake or something. There's more to life than sitting down and moping. I never moan, life is too short – the other day was a horrible day, wet and windy so I thought, what can I do today, I will go and visit somebody and make their life a bit happier.

Since Tony died, I've been on a cruise to the Mediterranean with Jane and to Corfu with both Julie and Jane, staying in a nice hotel.

In May 2023, I went to Edinburgh with my friend Carol Jenkins for four nights. We toured the Royal Yacht Britannia and visited various museums including the National Gallery and Edinburgh Castle and saw the special gardens there.

We also toured the city on an open-topped bus. We had a lovely time and the weather was really lovely, we were very lucky.

Della and Carol Jenkins on board the Royal Yacht Britannia.

I went to see the violinist André Rieu in July 2023 with Dianne Sissons in Maastricht, Holland, and we're going again this coming July, with my friend

Vanessa and Julie and Jane. Because I enjoyed it so much I wanted other people to enjoy it as well.

Della with Dianne Sissons at the André Rieu concert in Maastricht, Holland, in July 2023, with plans for a return trip in 2024.

In late November 2023 I attended the Royal Variety Show at the Royal Albert Hall with John, his wife Sarah and her mother Bernice Holman. I really enjoyed it, it was quite a spectacle.

It's different from when you see it on the television – it's much more spectacular, and the Duke and Duchess of Cambridge were there, with members of the Swedish royal family. They sat in the Royal Box and we had a good view of them.

Top: Della with Bernice Holman at the Royal Variety Show in November 2023 at the Royal Albert Hall. Below, in their seats for the show, from left: Bernice, Sarah, Della and John.

In January 2024 I had a very enjoyable week in Lanzarote with Jane and in April I went to Holland with Dianne Sissons to see the tulip fields.

Unfortunately, in the latter years with Tony, he couldn't manage to walk very far – he wasn't able to enjoy himself as much as he would have liked and he always felt guilty that he was probably stopping me going on holidays like I can now, although it never bothered me. But I can at least go away like this now.

The main thing is having something to look

forward to. Jane is also very keen for me to meet another gentleman and it's funny that Tony's sister's husband said the same. I think it would be rather nice to have somebody to go out for a meal with and go to stately homes and things like that – it's company, somebody my age with similar interests. And Tony would have approved, so we'll see!

Life goes on and you never know quite what is round the corner. There's always another chapter to be told!

APPENDIX

A LITTLE MORE ABOUT TONY

TONY Brookshaw sadly died while this book was being produced and this chapter is written in tribute to him and the full and happy life he led until his death on January 7th, 2022, at the age of 87, after a short illness.

His son John aptly summed up the kind of man Tony was at his funeral in Bangor-on-Dee in a moving eulogy: "Dad was a true entrepreneur and inspiration in equal measure, with a big dollop of humour and laughter thrown in. Over his lifetime he was a farmer, jockey, business owner, publican, pilot and drainage expert!"

Stanley Brookshaw

Anthony John Brookshaw was born on February 20th, 1934, in Shawbury, Shropshire, the youngest of four siblings.

His father was Stanley Brookshaw, a farmer, horse dealer and businessman who had married Mabel Alicia Bebbington, daughter of farmer, butcher and publican Tom Bebbington. Tony's oldest brother Thomas Peter (known as Peter) was born 11th March, 1927, followed by Stanley James (known as Tim) on 25th March, 1929. Then came his sister Mary Helena Lilly on 7th June, 1931, and finally Tony, just under three years later.

Tony's father Stan as a child sitting at the front on the right in this Edwardian family photo of the Brookshaws.

Tony as a child pushing a wheel-barrow on the lawn on the family farm at Aychley, Shrops.

Tony dressed as a page boy with his parents to attend a wedding.

Tim, Peter and Tony all grew up with a love of horse-riding – an exciting but dangerous pastime which tragically brought about Tim's premature death after an illustrious few years as one of Britain's leading jockeys.

His story is told in a meticulously-researched book by Chris Pitt who came over to The Plassey to interview Tony.

From Chris, we learn that while Peter and Tim were experts in gymkhanas, Tony preferred show ponies and enjoyed "conspicuous success" on a

Tony (right) as a pupil at Newport Grammar School.

horse named Friar's Balsam, which his father had bought for £1 as a foal.

Tony Brookshaw was the more academic of the three brothers and attended Adams Grammar School, Newport, which afforded a higher standard of education.

Tony with parents Mabel and Stan Brookshaw at brother Peter's wedding. Peter married Gwen Hough in the late 1940s, and Gwen's sister, Joan, married his brother Tim.

"I boarded at grammar school. I used to read books, my brothers didn't," Tony told Chris Pitt. "I read one about a young lad running away from school, so I ran away from school, twice. I walked about 13 miles.

"Peter was a good boy, Tim was a bit naughty. He was an absolute daredevil. I got on all right with Tim but Peter and Tim didn't get on from a young age. Peter was quite an aggressive chap, whereas Tim was much more friendly."

Brookshaw brothers Peter and Tim.

Tony excelled as a scholar but after leaving school, went back to work for his father at Aychley Farm in Market Drayton.

But in addition to farming, the Brookshaw children were learning another skill: horsemanship. As John Brookshaw noted in his eulogy for his father: "All the Brookshaw siblings were taught to ride almost before they could walk."

Tim, Peter and Tony all became successful jockeys with Tim going on to become a professional champion jockey. And Mary carried off many prizes in the show ring on her father's ponies.

There were some who thought Peter was possibly the best jockey out of them all, but Tony disagrees: "Tim was the better jockey," he insists. "I used to ride in races with Peter; Tim had turned professional by then. When Tim got on a horse he became part of the horse. I was a jockey on top of a horse but he was part and parcel of it. I once rode three winners in a day at Eyton point-to-point but I wasn't as good a rider as Tim or Peter. When Tim went hunting, the Master would be first over a fence but Tim would be right up there. He was fearless in his approach and that transmitted to the horse."

Tony on Friars Balsam as a child – the horse his father had bought as a foal for just one pound.

By 1959, all three brothers were skilled and experienced racing jockeys. That year, Tim rode three more winners at Bangor-on-Dee's two-day fixture on the 3rd and 4th April and Tony was first over the line at Bangor's hunter chase on Brockton, owned and trained by their father.

A racehorse by the name of Holly Bank was clearly a star performer for the Brookshaw family. The horse was bought by Stanley Brookshaw for £400, and Stanley hunted on him with Sir Watkin Williams Wynn. Holly Bank also won five prizes in the show ring before being put into training with Fred Rimmell.

Stanley Brookshaw on the middle horse, with Cecil Bromley, left, and Tony's sister Mary on the right.
Photograph courtesy of the Wellington Journal.

Over a nine-year period, the horse won 14 races, was placed in 14 more, and was ridden in all bar two of his 59 starts by one of the three Brookshaw brothers. Tony notched up six wins on Holly Bank, and Tim and Peter four apiece, including a big race at

Cheltenham. And Holly Bank successfully completed the 1958 Grand National with Peter in the saddle.

Tony took over as the horse's regular jockey from the 1958/59 season onwards, notes Chris, and it marked a return to form for the horse, with notable wins and placings over the next few months.

It was all looking promising for Tony to ride Holly Bank in the 1960 Grand National – but it wasn't to be.

As Tony recalled in conversation with Chris Pitt: "I was his regular jockey that year but I broke my leg at Warwick in January. A horse kicked me on the shinbone at the start. It caught me directly on the bone.

"I had to roll off the horse and get off the course so they could start the race. I'd have ridden him in that year's Grand National if I'd been fit. I did manage to ride in a point-to-point the week before the National but my leg wasn't right and I had to hop on one leg to the weighing room."

By the autumn, Tony had recovered and rode Holly Bank in a further eight races, scoring a final victory together in the Sedgley Handicap Chase at Wolverhampton on 27th December, 1960, taking the lead between the last two fences and holding on to prevail by a fast-diminishing neck.

Holly Bank turned 14 on New Year's Day, and his powers were waning. His last race was on April 24th 1961, after which he was retired to see out his days at The Plassey.

Tony with the cup for winning the Sir Watkin Williams Wyn Hunt Steeplechase in 1962 at Overton Hall, Malpas, for the second successive year on Holly Bank.

And Holly Bank's retirement coincided with Tony's withdrawal from racing. As mentioned earlier in the book, he and Della had got married in 1960 and were just at the start of their great adventure at The Plassey which began, of course, with the hard work of full-time farming.

Della had been quietly relieved that Tony decided to give up competitive horse-riding, mindful of the dangers it involved. Those dangers were well and truly spelt out three years later when Tim Brookshaw suffered a serious fall on 4th December, 1963 that left him partially paralysed.

Tony recalled: "We went to see him in hospital in Liverpool. My father was very worried about him. He pinched his leg but he didn't respond, there was no feeling."

With astonishing determination and fortitude, Tim Brookshaw eventually managed to ride again. But in November 1981 at the age of 52 he suffered another serious fall and this time, there were no second chances.

The accident happened at Lostford Manor Stables, near Ternhill, Shropshire. "A groom came to Tim and said that one of the horses was acting really funny," writes Chris Pitt. "Tim saddled the horse up and took him up the road for a steady gallop in the field. The horse reared up, stumbled and fell as he came back down, firing Tim over his head. As he lay on the ground, the horse got to his feet and kicked him in the back of the neck."

Tim Brookshaw was taken to Oswestry Orthopaedic Hospital where it was discovered he had two broken bones in his neck. For the second time in his life, he was paralysed.

Over the next few days pneumonia set in. Tim passed away shortly after 6am on Sunday, November 8th, 1981.

Above left: Tim Brookshaw on his wedding day in 1949
having just jumped down from an upstairs window(!) and,
above right, Tim with his daughter, Jill, in 1952.

As for Tony, with his horse-racing days behind him, and now a married man, his focus from 1960 onwards was on running The Plassey with his new bride, Della. And of course, the added challenge of fatherhood!

It was his father's "endless, drive and determination" together with his mother's ideas and suggestions, notes John Brookshaw, that saw The Plassey evolve from a mixed arable farm with a dairy and beef herd into what it is today – a hugely-successful leisure park and retail centre.

John believes that part of the inspiration for The Plassey was a film that his father absolutely loved: Carry On Camping. And, says John, "he delighted in modelling himself on the farmer in that film, Mr Josh Fiddler, leaning on the farmgate and telling Sid

James it was a pound to be a member; a pound for the booking fee and a pound for the tent, and so on.

"You could guarantee that whenever I was showing round VIPs and Park Inspectors, Dad would pop around the corner on his ATV with a cheeky grin and glint in his eyes, and shotgun across his lap, and recount the tale of Mr Fiddler. As ever, Dad's wicked sense of humour would reduce everyone to tears of laughter."

Tony at work at The Plassey on his ATV.

But in addition to a huge sense of fun, Tony Brookshaw had great drive and determination to take on projects and challenges and see them through. It was while Della was heavily pregnant and under doctor's orders to rest, that Tony "seized the opportunity" recalls John, to get on his bulldozer and start digging out the swimming pool – which has been a huge hit with holidaymakers to this day.

It was Tony who spearheaded other projects, including the Pitch & Putt Golf Course, creating fishing ponds and nature trails and also playing his part in the community through membership of the Wrexham Lions Club.

He organised and hosted many events at The Plassey that included gymkhanas, dance functions, fancy dress and even a Pram Race. In recognition of his achievements, Tony rose to become President of the Lions and in later years, Honorary Life member.

Tony drives a tractor pulling a raft for the raft race at Erbistock on an August bank holiday in the 1980s.

Another feature that was to prove hugely popular with caravanners was the Treetops Bar – a brainchild of Tony's, who liked nothing better than spending time in there serving pints to caravanners, and supping a few with them at the same time!

John recalls: "Dad would enjoy many a night often standing on top of the bar, singing such songs as The Blackbird Song and I've Got A Brand New Combine Harvester."

Tony loved getting behind the bar at Treetops – which has long proved to be a firm favourite of the caravanners.

Having hung up his saddle, Tony retained his thirst for adventure and to Della's alarm, took to flying microlight aircraft over The Plassey fields and caravan park – and lo and behold, with the inscription Tony and Della written in huge letters on the underside of the wings!

Tony prepares for take-off in his beloved microlight.

The hard work which Tony put into running The Plassey, with the constant support and companionship of his wife Della, was recognised over the years by a series of awards, from the Country Landowners' Association; Wales Tourist Board and numerous national awards for Britain's Best Holiday Park.

Holding a cup that he and Della were awarded for winning Best Site in North Wales in 1981.

John eloquently summed up the thoughts and feelings of the Brookshaw family at Tony's well-attended funeral with the closing words of his eulogy:

"Dad, we will miss you so much and words cannot describe the depth of loss we are all feeling. You were so kind, strong, generous, warm, fun-loving, gentle and incredibly hard-working man. But I know you would not want us to be sad, and instead would want us to celebrate what a fantastic and full life you have lived. We will certainly do this, Dad, and raise our glasses high in a toast to you, for your brilliant legacy called The Plassey, that you created for future generations to enjoy, and for giving us all so many wonderful, happy memories.

"You will forever be in our hearts."

At Tony's funeral service, a collection was made towards the Injured Jockeys Fund that was originally set up to support his brother Tim and fellow jockey Paddy Farrell after both sustained serious spinal injuries.

The plaque put up in Tony Brookshaw's honour on the wall outside his beloved folly. The Latin inscription reads:
Fortune Favours The Brave.

POSTSCRIPT

MY story has been told and I am now in the later stage of my life. I have looked back and relived my "three score years and ten," – although in my case, I've so far made it to four score years and five. As I write, I wonder how many years are left to me? Maybe there will still be another chapter to come in the years ahead!

Yes – it has been a great life. I have been happy and lucky – blessed with good parents and a very successful marriage – three good children and three wonderful grandchildren – a job in which I was fulfilled with good companionship.

And now, in retirement, great friendship.

Della Brookshaw

Printed in Great Britain
by Amazon

56439356R10116